Kissin' Wears Out Cookin' Don't

Past Recipes for Your Present and Future

Erica Oblinger-Mount

and

Donna J. McComas

SEABOARD PRESS

JAMES A. ROCK & COMPANY, PUBLISHERS

Kissin' Wears Out, Cookin' Don't: Past Recipes for Your Present and Future
by Erica Oblinger-Mount and Donna J. McComas

SEABOARD PRESS

is an imprint of JAMES A. ROCK & CO., PUBLISHERS

Kissin' Wears Out, Cookin' Don't: Past Recipes for Your Present and Future
copyright ©2009 by Erica Oblinger-Mount and Donna J. McComas

Special contents of this edition copyright ©2009 by Seaboard Press

Address comments and inquiries to:
SEABOARD PRESS
900 South Irby, #508
Florence, SC 29501

E-mail:
jrock@rockpublishing.com   lrock@rockpublishing.com
Internet URL: www.rockpublishing.com

Trade Paperback ISBN: 978-1-59663-706-1

Library of Congress Control Number: 2008929514

Printed in the United States of America

First Edition: 2009

This cookbook is dedicated to

the women

who fed us, loved us, and

molded us into

successful, caring adults

Virginia Marie Stevens

Eva "Tag" Oblinger

Ernestine McComas

Lucille Butcher

Lola Smith Adkins

Uncle Lanny's 9th birthday party, August 11, 1953.

Acknowledgments

A special thanks to our beloved family members, friends, & the internet for contributing recipes, advice, and wisdom in the compilation of this cookbook.

Mark A. McComas
Mike Mount
Amber Joy Oblinger
Claudia Stevens
Corky Lewis
Peg Oblinger
Maxine Hannon
Judy Mabe
Drema Goolsby
Randy Roy
Sis Tassen

Mauna Walden
Neva "Dee" Goolsby
Trisha Finley
Patsy Hazelrigg
Karen Thompson
Heather & Andrew Wagner
Kim Hammer
Dawn Schroeder
Kenneth E. Smith
Gerald Hartley
Marie Roberts

*Erica with her sister and cousins
having lunch at Mamaw Stevens' house.*

Contents

Introduction

Kissin' Wears Out, Cookin' Don't is a compilation of recipes from women who lived during the time when cooking at home was enjoyable, inexpensive, and always involved a family gathering. Money was spent on food and rarely on take-out. Restaurants & fast food establishments weren't on every street corner. It was a pretty routine situation. Dinner was served at a certain hour, usually 6:00, and if you were hungry, you were at the family table.

Tom Brokaw refers to this time as the "greatest generation." We refer to this time as "the greatest home cooking" by the matriarchs that we loved and remember fondly. Mothers, grandmothers, and aunts were all good cooks! Everyone met at the dinner table, said a prayer, ate, talked about work or school, and then the cleanup process began. It was a routine — a way of life.

Today, this type of family gathering only takes place during the holidays. Back in the day, it was a daily ritual. The dinner table meant family, good food, and a chance to share your day. *Kissin' Wears Out, Cookin' Don't* may not be the answer to getting the family together at the dinner table on a daily basis, but it certainly will bring back the "good home cooking" that we all sorely miss. And who knows, it might be the first step to starting your own family traditions.

Thanksgiving, 1970.

About the Authors

Erica Oblinger-Mount was born and raised in Huntington, West Virginia. She now resides in Charleston, South Carolina, with her wonderful husband, dog, and great friends. She graduated from Johnson & Wales University and is a co-founder of the Tanzanian Education Foundation. The love for cooking has always been a part of her life. She's married to a chef and is employed by a restaurant in Charleston. Although most of her spare time is spent working with her nonprofit foundation, she does enjoy reading, traveling, and cooking.

Donna J. McComas, mother, wife, and retired teacher, who was born and raised in Huntington, West Virginia. She has devoted most her time and energy to raising children and teaching in the public school system for 32 years. In her spare time, she enjoys reading, gardening & cooking, especially recipes that remind her of the "good old days." A special time when dinner was served sharply at 6:00, and the family was gathered at the dinner table. Every dish was home cooked and you never left a bite on your plate. Although her children are grown and she's retired from teaching, cooking seems to bring back those wonderful memories—even if it's just one meal at a time.

We may live without poetry, music, and art;
We may live without conscience and live without heart.
We may live without friends;
We may live without books.
But civilized man cannot live without cooks.
    —Owen Meredith
       Blue Ribbon Cookbook pub. 1986

And food for thought ...

Yesterday is history,
Tomorrow is a mystery,
And today?
Today is a gift.
That's why we call it the present.
    —Babatunde Olatunji
       Founder of the Voices of Africa Foundation

CHAPTER 1

Appetizers

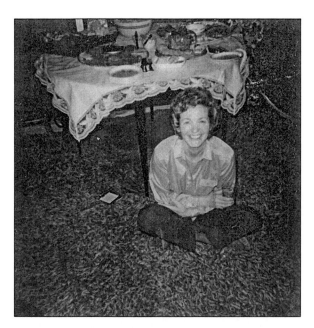

My mother, Virginia Stevens,
displaying her homemade appetizers.

Cookin' Notes

Salmon Ball

1   14.75-ounce can pink salmon

1   8-ounce package cream cheese

1   tablespoon minced onion

¼   teaspoon salt

1   tablespoon lemon juice (bottled or fresh)

1   teaspoon prepared horseradish

¼   teaspoon liquid smoke (optional)

Debone the pink salmon. Crumble salmon into a bowl. Mix the remaining ingredients. Refrigerate 4 hours. Roll in parsley. Serve with favorite crackers.

Note: While crumbling salmon, check for hidden small bones.

Bologna Spread

2   pounds chunk bologna

1   16-ounce package American cheese

8   boiled eggs

sweet pickle relish (to taste)

mayonnaise (to add moisture)

Grind the first 3 ingredients together. Add pickle relish to taste. Add mayonnaise for moisture. Serve with favorite crackers or as mini-sandwiches.

Servings: 20-25

Note: Recipe may be divided to accommodate fewer than 20-25 persons.

Supreme Chicken Spread

2/3　cup mayonnaise

2　tablespoons vinegar

1　teaspoon salt

4-5　cups cut-up, cooked chicken or turkey

1　cup celery, chopped

1　cup sweet pickle relish or 1 cup minced green pepper

2　teaspoons onion, grated

2/3　cup chopped walnuts or pecans

In a large bowl with fork, combine mayonnaise, vinegar and salt. Add chicken and remaining ingredients; mix well. Cover and refrigerate for 1 hour.

Note: Chicken spread can be served on bread, with crackers, on a bed of lettuce, or as a filling. Turkey can be substituted for chicken.

Sausage Balls

1　pound mild or hot sausage

2　cups Bisquick mix

½　cup water

1　12-ounce package sharp cheddar cheese

Mix ingredients together. Form into balls. Bake on cookie sheet for 12-15 minutes at 400 degrees.

History: Bisquick became a popular cooking item beginning in 1931.

Sausage Stuffed Mushrooms

20 fresh mushrooms

1 pound mild or hot sausage

4 teaspoons onions, grated

½ cup bread crumbs

1 teaspoon salt

½ teaspoon pepper

Fry sausage. Remove from pan and pat with a paper towel. Crumble sausage. Wash mushrooms. Remove stems and reserve caps. Chop stems and mix with crumbled sausage, onions, bread crumbs, salt, and pepper. Fill mushroom caps with mixture. Bake at 350 degrees for 20 minutes.

Serves: 8-10

Tip: Aluminum will discolor light-colored mushrooms.

Cheese Crisps

1½ cups sharp cheddar cheese

½ cup softened butter

1 cup sifted flour

½ teaspoon salt

¼ teaspoon red pepper flakes

½ cup finely chopped pecans

Grate cheese. Blend cheese and butter. Add flour, salt, and red pepper. Mix thoroughly. Stir in chopped pecans. With floured hands, shape mixture into two rolls (1 inch diameter). Wrap in wax paper and chill for at least 2 hours. After chilled, slice thin. Bake on ungreased cookie sheet for 8 minutes at 350 degrees. Let cool.

Servings: 30

Bacon-Wrapped Water Chestnuts

1½   pounds sliced bacon

3   8-ounce cans whole water chestnuts, drained and halved

1½   cups brown sugar, packed

¾   cup ketchup

¾   cup mayonnaise

Cut bacon strips into thirds. Wrap each strip around a halved water chestnut and secure with a toothpick. Place in an ungreased 13 x 9 inch glass dish. Bake uncovered at 400 degrees for 30-35 minutes or until bacon is crisp. Turn chestnuts once during baking. Drain. Combine the brown sugar, ketchup, and mayonnaise. Pour over water chestnuts. Bake 6-8 minutes longer or until bubbly.

Servings: 8½ dozen

Modern name of dish: Rumaki
Note: Bacon wrapped water chestnuts can be served with sweet & sour sauce instead of brown sugar, ketchup, and mayonnaise topping.

Pepperoni Bread

1   loaf frozen bread (24-ounces)

1   tablespoon butter

1½   cups shredded mozzarella cheese

1½   cups pepperoni, sliced thin (or 2 8-ounce packages pepperoni)

1   beaten egg

Let bread thaw and rise. Roll flat. Top with butter, cheese, and pepperoni slices. Roll up like a jellyroll. Spread beaten egg over roll and seal. Bake on cookie sheet or in a loaf pan at 350 degrees for 25-30 minutes. Serve hot.

Tip: Preheat pepperoni for 1 minute in microwave to release the fat before using in any recipe.

Meatballs with Sauce

  1 pound ground beef, chuck, or sirloin
  ½ cup bread crumbs
  1/3 cup minced onion
  ¼ cup milk
  1 egg
  1 tablespoon parsley flakes
  1 teaspoon salt
  1/8 teaspoon pepper
  ½ teaspoon Worcestershire sauce

Mix all ingredients thoroughly in a bowl. Shape into 1 inch balls. Bake for 20 minutes at 375 degrees. Put meatballs in a crock pot and cover with sauce. Gently stir meatballs and sauce. Cook on low heat for 1 hour or until sauce is hot.

Meatball Sauce

  ½ cup ketchup
  ½ cup of bottled chili sauce
  1/8 cup vinegar
  1 teaspoon Worcestershire sauce
  2 tablespoons brown sugar

Mix all ingredients together. Pour over meatballs.

Crock Pot Meatballs

1   16-ounce package frozen meatballs

1   20-ounce bottle Heinz 57 sauce

1   32-ounce jar grape jelly

Put sauce & jelly in a crock pot. Mix thoroughly. Add meatballs. Stir gently. Turn crock pot on high setting for 2 hours. Serve hot.

History: In 1971, Rival trademarked the crock pot.

Egg Rolls

¼   cup vegetable oil

1   pound lean pork, cubed

½   pound frozen raw shrimp, shelled, deveined, chopped

4   cups bean sprouts

2   cups celery, chopped

8   green onions, chopped

1   teaspoon salt

1   tablespoon cornstarch

2   tablespoons bottled soy sauce

1   12-ounce package egg roll wrappers

1   egg, beaten

    oil for frying in deep fryer

Heat vegetable oil in wok or skillet. Add pork. Cook until pork is done. Add shrimp. Cook for 1 minute. Add vegetables and salt. Cook 2 minutes, stirring frequently. Sprinkle with cornstarch; mix well. Stir in soy sauce. Cook for 1 minute. Pour into colander; set aside until cool. Put 2-3 tablespoons of cooled filling in egg roll skin, slightly below center. Brush edges with beaten egg. Fold 1 corner over filling. Fold 2 opposite corners toward center. Roll toward remaining corner to form a cylinder. Continue filling egg roll skins in the same fashion. Fry in deep fryer at 375 degrees until golden brown. Drain.

Note: May cut rolls in half to make mini-egg rolls.
Suggestion: Serve with duck sauce or hot mustard.

Crab Cakes

2   pounds lump crabmeat

3   egg whites, whipped

2   cups mayonnaise

5   green onions, chopped

2   tablespoons lemon juice

¾   cup cracker crumbs (saltines)

¼   cup parsley, chopped

1   teaspoon salt

1   pinch cayenne pepper

¼   teaspoon creole seasoning

    vegetable oil (amount varies)

Whip egg whites. Add mayonnaise, lemon juice, chopped green onions, parsley, salt, cayenne pepper, creole seasoning, and cracker crumbs. Fold crabmeat into mixture. Form into patties. Cover frying pan with a coating of vegetable oil. Place crab cakes in pan and fry 3-4 minutes on each side or until golden brown. Put on paper towels for absorption of oil before plating. May need to coat pan several times with oil in order to fry all the crab cakes (depends on the size of the frying pan).

Serves: Approx. 11 six-ounce crab cakes

Tip: Microwave a lemon for 1 minute & it will produce twice the amount of juice.

Chicken Liver Pâté

12 tablespoons butter (1½ sticks)
 1 small onion, finely chopped
 1 small green apple, peeled, cored, thinly sliced
 1 pound chicken livers
¼ cup apple brandy or cognac
 1 teaspoon salt
 1 teaspoon black pepper
1/3 cup heavy cream

Heat 3 tablespoons of butter in a small pan. Add the onion and apple and fry slowly until softened but not browned. Add the chicken livers. Increase the heat and fry for 5 minutes. The livers should remain quite pink in the center. Add the brandy or cognac and light it with a match. When the flames have died down, transfer these ingredients and all the remaining ingredients to a blender. Process until smooth. Pour into a large serving dish. Chill for 4 hours.

Serve with your favorite crackers.

Note: Pâté is heavier than mousse which has a much lighter texture.

Pineapple Cheese Ball

1 8-ounce package Philadelphia Cream Cheese

½ medium green pepper, finely chopped

½ medium onion, finely chopped

3 tablespoons canned crushed pineapple

1 cup finely chopped nuts (walnuts or pecans)

Soften cream cheese to room temperature. Add next 3 ingredients and mix thoroughly. Chill until firm. Shape into a ball and roll in finely chopped nuts.

Serve with favorite crackers.

Note: Pineapples can weigh up to 20 pounds.

Chipped Beef Cheese Ball

1 8-ounce package of Philadelphia Cream Cheese

4 green onions with blades, finely chopped

2 teaspoons Worcestershire sauce

1 teaspoon soy sauce

½ teaspoon Accent Seasoning

1 4.5-ounce jar chipped beef

Mix cream cheese, chopped onions, both sauces, seasoning, and 1/3 package of chipped beef thoroughly. Roll mixture into a ball then roll cheese ball into the remaining chipped beef. Refrigerate overnight.

Serve with favorite crackers.

Quatro Cheese Ball

2   8-ounce packages Philadelphia Cream Cheese, softened
½   pound Swiss cheese, shredded
¼   pound cheddar cheese, shredded
2   ounces bleu cheese, crumbled
2   teaspoons Worcestershire sauce
1   small onion, grated
½   teaspoon salt
1   teaspoon mustard
1   teaspoon horseradish
2   teaspoons sweet pickle relish, drained
½   cup chopped pecans
½   cup parsley flakes

Combine all ingredients except the chopped pecans and parsley flakes.
Mix thoroughly and chill. Shape into 1 large cheese ball or 2 small
cheese balls. Roll in a mixture of chopped pecans and parsley flakes.
Serve at room temperature with assorted crackers.

Tip: Almonds can be substituted in any recipe calling for nuts.
   23 almonds = 1-ounce serving

Chili Cheese Ball

1   8-ounce package cream cheese

1   8-ounce container cheese spread

½   teaspoon garlic powder

¼   teaspoon red pepper flakes

1   teaspoon paprika

1   teaspoon chili powder

Mix first 4 ingredients together thoroughly. Form a ball with the mixture. Roll cheese ball into the mixed paprika and chili powder. Chill until firm.

History: Philadelphia brand cream cheese went on sale in 1885.

Jalapeno Pepper Cheese Ball

1   10¾-ounce can bean with bacon soup

4   cups shredded sharp cheddar cheese

2/3   cup jalapeno relish or chopped green chiles

1   cup chopped parsley flakes or pecans

Mix soup, cheese, and relish together in a bowl with electric mixer. Beat until smooth; chill. On wax paper, shape mixture into 4 logs (4"x 1½"); roll in chopped parsley flakes or pecans.

Serve with crackers.

Serving: Makes 4 logs or 60 appetizer servings.
History: Campbell's invented condensed soup in 1897.

Vegetable Dip

   1   cup mayonnaise
   ½   cup sour cream
   1/3 cup diced green pepper
   1/3 cup diced radishes
   ¼   teaspoon onion salt

Combine ingredients. Mix well. Serve with carrot sticks, zucchini slices, cherry tomatoes, broccoli flowerettes, celery sticks, or potato chips.

Yields: 2 cups

Taco Dip

   1½ pounds ground beef
   1   small onion, chopped
   1   package taco seasoning (1-ounce)
   1   16-ounce can refried beans
   1   8-ounce package shredded cheddar cheese

Fry ground beef, onion, taco seasoning, and refried beans. Drain & put in a serving dish. Top with shredded cheddar cheese (will melt on its own).

Side dishes: sour cream & salsa

Fruit Dip

1 8-ounce container Cool Whip
½ cup pineapple juice
1 cup sugar
1 egg, well beaten
1 teaspoon flour
   pinch of salt
½ teaspoon vanilla
1 teaspoon almond extract

Combine sugar, flour, and salt in saucepan. Mix. Add pineapple juice and well-beaten egg. Cook on medium-low heat until it thickens; stirring constantly. Remove from heat; add butter and flavorings. Cool mixture. Fold in Cool Whip. Refrigerate.

Tip: Fruit dip can be frozen and used at a later date.

Spicy Chip Dip

2 8-ounce packages cream cheese
¼ cup yellow mustard
¼ cup ketchup
1 tablespoon onion juice
1 tablespoon garlic wine vinegar
1 tablespoon Worcestershire sauce
½ teaspoon Tabasco sauce

Mix well. Serve at room temperature.

Fruit Pizza

1   16.5-ounce roll refrigerated sugar cookie dough

1   8-ounce package cream cheese

6   tablespoons sugar

    Strawberry Glaze

    whipped cream, optional

    Fruit (sliced): strawberries, peaches, cherries, pineapple,
       grapes, cantaloupe

Roll cookie dough thinly & place on pizza pan. Bake dough 15 minutes on 375 degrees or until golden brown. Let cool. Mix cream cheese & sugar; spread on cooled crust. Spread pie glaze over top. Add choice of sliced fruit on crust. Keep refrigerated until ready to serve. Top with whipped cream, if desired.

Strawberry Glaze

1   cup granulated sugar

3   tablespoons strawberry Jello

3   tablespoons cornstarch

1   cup water

In a saucepan, mix all the ingredients together. Cook on medium heat for 5 minutes or until glaze is clear & thick. Stir frequently. If too thick, add 1-2 additional teaspoons of water. Brush on fruit.

Sweet Potato Pancakes

1 cup self-rising flour

2 tablespoons sugar

1/8 teaspoon ground cinnamon

1/8 ground clove

2/3 cup cooked sweet potatoes, mashed

1 tablespoon butter, melted

1¼ cups milk

Mix together flour, sugar, and spices in a large bowl. In 2nd bowl, combine sweet potatoes, butter, and milk; mix until well blended. Combine both mixtures together until blended smoothly. Spray griddle or pan with nonstick cooking spray. For each pancake, drop 3 tablespoons batter on griddle. Cook until both sides are brown. Serve with pancake syrup or applesauce.

Yields: 8-10 pancakes

Salmon Popovers

1 11-ounce box 2-pie crust mix

1 14.75-ounce can pink salmon, drained

1 tablespoon mayonnaise

1 teaspoon lemon juice (fresh or bottled)

¼ teaspoon paprika

Prepare pastry. Roll out and cut into 12 four inch squares. Set aside. Drain salmon. Remove skin & bones from salmon. Break into small pieces. Add mayonnaise and lemon juice. Place 1 tablespoon of mixture on each 4" square. Moisten edges of square with water; fold into triangles. Press edges together; make a small slice on top of each triangle for venting. Bake at 425 degrees until golden brown.

Serves: 4-5

Pineapple Dip

 1 pineapple
 1 cup shredded cheddar cheese
 1 8-ounce package cream cheese
 ½ cup milk
 2 tablespoons Worcestershire sauce
 1 tablespoon scallion tops, finely sliced

Cut pineapple in half crosswise and remove meat from the bottom half making a shell to be used later. Cut pineapple meat into cubes removing the seeded middle pieces. Mix together the cream cheese, milk, scallion, cheddar cheese and Worcestershire sauce. Place this mixture in shell and refrigerate. Use the top of the pineapple and slice in order to get the most meat possible. Cut into chunks and chill. Allow cream cheese mix in pineapple to soften for approximately 20 minutes before serving.

Tip: A fresh pineapple has deep green leaves.

Bleu Cheese Party Dip

1/3 cup ketchup
 3 tablespoons milk
 ½ teaspoon prepared horseradish
 ¼ teaspoon salt
 1 8-ounce package cream cheese (softened)
1/3 cup crumbled bleu cheese

Mix the ingredients together; cover and chill before serving. Makes 1½ cups.

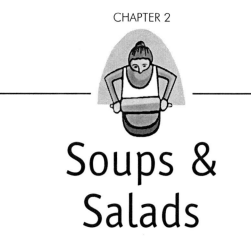

CHAPTER 2

Soups & Salads

Mamaw Tag & the Lewis family enjoying a family picnic.

Cookin' Notes

Mark's Incredible Vegetable Beef Soup

1   pound ground sirloin or ground chuck

1   pound stew beef chunks

2   28-ounce cans diced tomatoes

1   8-ounce can tomato sauce

2   14-ounce cans beef broth

3   slices bacon

½   package baby carrots

½   small head cabbage

2   stalks celery

1   8-ounce can peas

1   8-ounce can corn

2   4-ounce cans mushrooms

1   8-ounce can green beans

2   large potatoes

1   tablespoon sugar

Prep: Chop onions, cabbage, celery, and potatoes.

In large soup pot, add onions, ground sirloin or ground chuck, and stew beef chunks and brown. Once browned, add 2 cups water and bring to a boil; simmer for 5 minutes and then drain off water and oil. In same pan, add diced tomatoes, tomato sauce, two 8-ounce cans beef broth and 3 slices bacon. Bring to a boil and simmer for 20 minutes, stirring occasionally. Next, add baby carrots, cabbage, and celery. Simmer for 1 hour. Add the (undrained) peas, corn, mushrooms, and green beans. Add chopped potatoes and sugar. Simmer for 40 minutes, stirring occasionally. Add salt and pepper to taste. If more liquid is needed, add remaining beef broth.

Tip: A leaf of lettuce dropped into the pot, absorbs the grease from the top of the soup. Remove the lettuce & throw it away as soon as it serves its purpose.

Hot and Cheesy Potato Soup

5   pounds potatoes

3   stalks celery

3   onions

3   carrots

1   teaspoon celery salt

8   ounces Velveeta cheese

5   ounces mild Mexican Velveeta cheese

1   6-ounce can Carnation cream

1   stick butter

    salt and pepper to taste

Prep: Chop potatoes, celery, onions, and carrots.

In large soup pot, cook potatoes, onions, celery, and carrots for 30 minutes. Add salt and pepper to taste. Remove from burner and add remaining ingredients. Allow the cheese to melt, stirring occasionally. When ingredients are combined, mix well and serve.

History: Velveeta cheese was produced in 1928.

Cream of Potato Soup

8 ounces peeled potatoes

1 large onion, chopped

1 bay leaf

1 14-ounce can chicken broth or water

2 tablespoons butter for white sauce

1 tablespoon butter (mix with cream)

1 ounce flour

½ pint milk

¼ cup cream or evaporated milk

   salt & pepper to taste

   cayenne pepper, as a garnish

   chopped watercress, if desired, as a garnish

Simmer the potatoes and onion with the bay leaf in the broth until soft. Rub through a sieve. Make a white sauce of butter, flour, and milk. Add the pureed potatoes. Stir in cream and the 1 tablespoon of butter. Heat gently. Season well. Garnish with cayenne pepper and chopped watercress, if desired.

Tip: Soup should be cooked gently. Remember the maxim: Soup boiled is soup spoiled.

French Onion Soup

    3 tablespoons butter
    1 tablespoon vegetable oil
    6 cups onion, sliced thin
    ½ teaspoon salt
    ½ teaspoon sugar
  1/8 teaspoon pepper
    3 tablespoons flour
    5 14-ounce cans beef broth
    1 loaf French bread (24-ounces)
   2½ cups mozzarella cheese

In large soup pot (4-6 quarts), heat butter and oil over medium heat.
When butter is melted, add onions and sauté for about 15 minutes.
Add salt, pepper, and sugar. Increase heat to medium high and cook for
30-40 minutes. Stir every 2 or 3 minutes scraping bottom of pot until
onions are a deep nutty brown. Sprinkle browned onions with flour.
Add 2 cans beef broth, stirring constantly until well-blended. Add
remaining cans beef broth. Partially cover and simmer for 1½ hours.
Before serving, pre-heat oven to 375 degrees. Slice French bread and
arrange a layer over soup. Sprinkle with cheese. Bake for 20 minutes
and then broil for 2-3 minutes or until cheese is lightly browned.

Yields: 6 cups

Tip: Peel onion under water or in draft to prevent crying.

Tag's Hearty Ham Chowder

4	large potatoes, diced
2	tablespoons butter
¼	cup green onions, sliced
½	cup green peppers, chopped
2	cups water
1	teaspoon salt
1/8	teaspoon white pepper
¼	teaspoon paprika
3	tablespoons flour
½	cup cold water
2	cups milk
1	12-ounce can whole kernel corn (undrained)
2	cups diced cooked ham
2	tablespoons parsley

Prep: Dice green onions, green peppers, and cooked ham. Peel & dice potatoes.

In large soup pot, melt butter. Add onions and green peppers. Cook until tender (but not brown.) Add 2 cups of water, salt, white pepper, and paprika. Cover and simmer until potatoes are tender. Make a paste with flour and cold water. Blend into potato mixture. Add milk and cook, stirring until slightly thickened. Stir in corn and ham. Heat thoroughly. Before serving, sprinkle with chopped parsley.

Yields: 6 servings

Tip: If parsley is washed with hot water instead of cold, it retains its flavor & is easier to chop.

Chicken Gumbo

- 2 tablespoons oil
- 2 tablespoons flour
- 2 slices cooked bacon, diced
- 1 cup onions, chopped
- 1 cup green peppers, chopped
- 2 cloves garlic, chopped
- 1 teaspoon salt
- 1 teaspoon black pepper
- 1 teaspoon Worcestershire sauce
- 1 teaspoon red pepper seasoning
- 1 16-ounce can stewed tomatoes
- 4 whole chicken breasts; halved
- 4 cups water
- 1 16-ounce bag frozen okra
- 2 cups rice (see Rice Recipe next page)

Prep: Chop onions, green pepper, and garlic cloves. Cook and dice bacon.

In large soup pot, combine oil and flour and cook until brown. Add bacon and cook thoroughly. Then add onion, green pepper, and garlic. Cook 4-5 minutes. Add salt, pepper, Worchestshire sauce, red pepper seasoning, tomatoes, chicken and water. Let simmer for 45 minutes to an hour. Remove chicken breasts from soup; debone and remove skins. Cut meat into small pieces. Remove fat from surface of liquid; bring to boil. Add okra, stirring occasionally for 15 minutes. Return chicken to mixture and heat. Serve over rice.

Serves: 4

Rice Recipe

2 4-ounce cans mushrooms

7 stalks green onions, chopped

2 teaspoons oregano

2 tablespoons olive oil

1 teaspoon salt

2 cups rice (uncooked)

3 cups beef broth

2 cups hot water

Preheat oven at 450 degrees. Add olive oil to pan and heat. Add mushrooms, green onions, oregano, and salt. Sauté until slightly browned. Add rice, beef broth, and water to mixture. Remove to baking dish; bake for 1 hour uncovered.

Tip: One cup of uncooked long grain white rice equals 3 cups cooked rice.

Chicken Noodle Soup

1   chicken, 3-4 pounds

3   quarts water

1   carrot, diced

2   stalks celery, chopped

1   medium onion, chopped

1   tablespoon salt

¼   teaspoon pepper

½   package egg noodles (approximately 6-ounces)

Cook chicken in water until tender; approximately 60 minutes. Add onion, carrot, celery, salt, and pepper. Cook 1 hour. Strain soup; reserve as stock. Debone & remove skin from chicken. After cooling, cut chicken into bite-size chunks. Return chicken & stock to pot. Add seasoning. Put egg noodles in pot & continue cooking for 10 minutes or until noodles are done. May need to add more water to soup pot. Serve hot.

Serves: 6

Tip: Cooked chicken will be crispier if drained on a metal rack or a brown paper bag.

Hamburger Soup

1   pound ground sirloin

1   onion, chopped

2   potatoes, chopped

1   16-ounce package frozen mixed vegetables

1   14-ounce can stewed Italian-style tomatoes

2   14-ounce cans beef broth

1   teaspoon oregano

Prep: Chop onion and potatoes.

Brown ground sirloin in skillet and then drain fat. In a large soup pot, add cooked meat and all remaining ingredients. Bring to a boil. Once boiling, reduce heat & let simmer for 25 minutes. Serve hot.

Homemade Chili

1 15-ounce can pinto beans

1 15-ounce can light red kidney beans (with liquid)

1 15-ounce can Great Northern beans (with liquid)

1 28-ounce can diced tomatoes (or a quart canned tomatoes)

2 pounds ground chuck

1 large onion, diced

1 2.25-ounce package French's Chili-O

½ teaspoon salt

½ teaspoon pepper

½ teaspoon red pepper flakes

1 teaspoon chili powder, optional

1 teaspoon sugar

water (if necessary)

hot sauce, optional

sour cream, optional

Fry ground chuck and onion in a skillet for 20 minutes or until done. Drain; put in a large stock pot. Add the remaining ingredients to pot & stir thoroughly. Cook on medium heat for 40 minutes. Thin soup with water, if too thick. Cook for 15 minutes longer until heated thoroughly. Serve with saltines.

Suggestion: May top each bowl with a dollop of sour cream or favorite hot sauce.

Chicken Salad with a Twist

1   16-ounce package rotini pasta

3   cups cooked chicken, cut in small pieces

½   cup Italian dressing

1½   cups mayonnaise

3   tablespoons lemon juice

1   tablespoon mustard

1   medium onion, chopped

1   cup cucumber, chopped

1   cup celery, chopped

1   teaspoon pepper

1   teaspoon salt

Prep: Chop onion, cucumbers, and celery. Cook pasta and keep hot. Cook chicken and cut into small pieces.

In a large bowl, mix cooked chicken, Italian dressing, hot pasta, mayonnaise, and lemon juice. Mix thoroughly. Add mustard, onion, cucumbers, celery, pepper, and salt to taste. Mix thoroughly; chill for 2 hours.

Tip: Use chilled ingredients in salads using chicken or cooked meat.

Old Fashioned Ham and Macaroni Salad

2 cups cooked elbow macaroni

2 cups cooked ham, chopped

1½ cups shredded cheddar cheese

½ cup chopped green pepper

1/3 cup chopped onion

½ cup mayonnaise

2 tablespoons milk

2 tablespoons white vinegar

½ tablespoon salt

Prep: Cook macaroni according to directions on box; drain. Chop cooked ham, green pepper, and onion.

In large bowl, combine macaroni, ham, cheese, green pepper, and onion. Stir well; chill for 30 minutes. In separate bowl, combine mayonnaise, milk, vinegar, and salt. Pour over chilled macaroni mixture; toss well.

Servings: 10

Tip: If using blocks of cheese; chill cheese to grate more easily.

7 Layer Salad

1	head lettuce
1	onion, chopped
1	16-ounce package frozen peas
10	slices bacon (cooked and chopped)
1	8-ounce package shredded cheddar cheese
2	green peppers chopped
2	medium tomatoes, chopped
2	carrots, shredded
1½	cups mayonnaise
1	teaspoon sugar
	salt and pepper to taste

Prep: Chop lettuce, onion, green peppers, and tomatoes. Shred carrots. Cook and chop bacon.

In a large salad bowl, layer:

Lettuce, carrots, onions, frozen peas, crumbled bacon, cheese, green peppers, and tomatoes (Do Not Toss.) In a separate bowl, mix mayonnaise, salt, pepper, and sugar. Spread mixture on top of salad. Cover and refrigerate at least 8 hours. Toss before serving.

Tip: Lettuce keeps better if stored in the refrigerator dry. Wash the day of usage.

Spinach Salad

    1 16-ounce bag torn spinach
    1 8-ounce can water chestnuts (drained)
    2 hard boiled eggs, chopped
    1 3.25-ounce jar bacon bits
       Feta cheese (7-ounces)
    1 small onion, cut in rings
   10 fresh mushrooms, sliced
    1 cup salad oil
   ½ cup red wine vinegar
   ½ cup sugar
  1/3 cup ketchup
       dash of salt

Prep: Cut onions into rings, slice mushrooms, and chop hard boiled eggs.

Dressing: Mix salad oil, red wine vinegar, sugar, ketchup, and dash of salt. Stir thoroughly.

In a large bowl, add torn spinach, water chestnuts, eggs, bacon bits, Feta cheese, onion, and sliced mushrooms; toss. Pour dressing over salad and serve.

Tip: Use a wet knife to slice a hard boiled egg.

Green Bean Salad

2 14.5-ounce cans French style green beans

1 15-ounce can green peas

½ cup chopped celery

1 cup white vinegar

1 cup sugar

½ cup oil

chopped onion and green pepper to taste

salt and pepper to taste

Prep: Chop celery, onion, and green peppers.

Drain green beans and peas; put in a large bowl. Add all ingredients; let marinate overnight. When ready to serve, drain.

Tip: Celery wrapped in aluminum foil will last longer.

Kraut Salad

1   14-ounce can kraut

1   4-ounce can pimento

1   medium onion, chopped

2   cups celery, chopped

1   cup green peppers, chopped

¾   cup sugar

1   cup water

¼   cup oil

½   cup white vinegar

1   teaspoon salt

Prep: Chop onion, celery, and green pepper.

In large bowl, mix kraut, pimento, onion, celery, and green pepper. In a separate bowl, mix sugar, water, oil, vinegar, and salt. Mix well; pour over kraut mixture. Let stand for 45 minutes. When ready to serve, drain.

Tip: Do not use metal bowl when mixing salads. Use wooden, glass, or china bowls.

Linguini Salad

1 pound box linguini

1 cucumber, chopped

1 green pepper, chopped

2 tomatoes, chopped

1 16-ounce bottle Italian dressing

1 6-ounce bottle McCormick's Salad Supreme

Prep: Cook pasta according to directions; drain. Chop cucumbers, green peppers, and tomatoes.

Mix all ingredients together; refrigerate for 24 hours.

Tip: Add a little oil when cooking linguini & it won't boil over or stick together.

History: Pasta was produced commercially in the United States in 1848.

Pot Luck Cabbage Salad

- 2   cups cider vinegar
- 1   cup sugar
- 2   tablespoons salt
- 1   green pepper, chopped
- 2   red peppers, chopped
- 2   onions, chopped
- 10 cups cabbage, thinly sliced
- ½   teaspoon ground turmeric
- ¾   teaspoon celery seed
- 1   tablespoon mustard seed

Prep: Slice cabbage; chop onions, green peppers, and red peppers.

In a saucepan, add cider vinegar, sugar, salt, mustard seed, celery seed, and turmeric. Bring to a boil, then reduce heat and simmer for 5 minutes. In a large bowl, mix cabbage, onions, and peppers. Pour vinegar over vegetables and stir to coat. Cover and refrigerate overnight.

Tip: Use 1/3 the amount of dried herbs as you would fresh herbs in a recipe.

Cornbread Salad

2 8.5-ounce boxes Jiffy Cornbread Mix

1 cup mayonnaise

1 tablespoon mustard

1 green pepper, chopped

1 tomato, chopped

1 cucumber, chopped

½ onion, chopped

Prep: Chop green pepper, tomato, cucumber, and onion.

Bake cornbread according to directions on box. Crumble cornbread after cooling. Mix together all vegetables in separate bowl and then add to cornbread. Mix in mayonnaise and mustard. Add salt and pepper to taste. Refrigerate for 2 hours before serving.

Note: You may want to add more mayonnaise/mustard if mixture is too dry.

History: Mabel White Holmes developed and introduced to the homemaker the first prepared baking mix product in the spring of 1930. Currently, 21 Jiffy mixes are available to the consumer. (Source: Jiffy website)

Carrot Salad

2 1 pound packages carrots, shredded

1 cup miniature marshmallows

1 16-ounce can crushed pineapple, juice included

¼ cup confectioner's sugar

1 teaspoon vanilla flavoring

½ cup raisins

Mix all ingredients together. Keep in refrigerator until ready to serve.

Tip: Raisins need to be refrigerated in an airtight container. Raisins do freeze well.

Wilted Lettuce

5 slices bacon, crisp & finely chopped

4 tablespoons bacon fat drippings

1 teaspoon salt

2-3 green onions, chopped

2 tablespoons vinegar

batch leaf lettuce

Fry bacon until crisp. Remove from skillet & place on paper towels; drain. Remove skillet off heat until later. Measure fat drippings; will need at least 4 tablespoons for salad topping. Return drippings to skillet. Tear lettuce into pieces and place in a salad bowl. Add chopped onions. Season with salt. Return skillet with bacon grease to heat until hot. Spread drippings over greens and onions. Crumble crisp bacon over top. Serve immediately.

Triple Orange Salad

2 cups boiling water

1 3.5-ounce package orange Jello

1 pint orange sherbet

2 14.5-ounce cans mandarin oranges

1 13.5-ounce can pineapple chunks

1 cup flaked coconut

1 cup miniature marshmallows

½ cup whipped cream

Mix boiling water and Jello; stir until fully dissolved. Add sherbet and mix well. Add drained mandarin oranges; pour into 6 cup mold. In separate bowl, mix the other can of drained mandarin oranges & pineapple chunks, coconut flakes, and marshmallows. Fold in whipped cream; chill for 3 hours. Unmold Jello and fill center with whipped cream mixture. Serve immediately.

Winter Fruit Salad

1   20-ounce can pineapple chunks in natural juices

1   4.6-ounce box cook & serve vanilla pudding

1   quart mixed fresh fruit chunks (apples, bananas, oranges, pears, etc)

¾   cup chopped pecans or walnuts

1/3   cup flaked coconut

    whipped cream, optional

Drain pineapple; reserve juice. Set pineapple aside. In a saucepan, combine pineapple juice and pudding mix; cook over medium heat until thickened. Cool. Combine pineapple chunks and other fruit, nuts, and coconut in large bowl; mix thoroughly. Add pudding mixture; stir to coat. Chill until ready to serve. Garnish with whipped topping, if desired.

Makes: 6-8 servings

Note: 20-ounce can = 10 cored pineapple slices

Holiday Salad

1½ cups hot water
 1 3.5-ounce package lime Jello
 1 13.5-ounce can crushed pineapple
 1 small package marshmallows
 ½ carton whipped cream
 1 cup chopped pecans

Mix Jello and hot water; stir until dissolved. Cool. Add juice from
pineapple; let stand until it begins to thicken. Add pineapple,
marshmallows, and nuts. Chill for 3 hours. Cut into squares; top with
whipped cream.

Serves: 9-10

Concealed Cranberry Salad

 1 3.4-ounce package cherry flavored Jello
 1 16-ounce can jellied cranberry sauce
 1 cup apples, diced
 1 cup boiling water
 1 13.5-ounce can crushed pineapples
 ½ cup chopped nuts

Dissolve cherry Jello in boiling water. Put cranberry sauce through
sieve; add hot mixture. Place mixture over ice water until Jello begins
to thicken. Add pineapple, apples, and nuts to mixture. Pour into
individual or large mold. Place in refrigerator until firm.

Pineapple Cracker Salad

6   egg whites

2   teaspoons baking powder

2   cups sugar

2   cups crushed Ritz crackers

2   packages Dream Whip

1   8-ounce package cream cheese

1   20-ounce can crushed pineapple (drained)

1   cup coconut, flaked

Preheat oven 350 degrees. Mix egg whites, baking powder, sugar, and crackers. Place in baking pan. Bake for 20 minutes. In separate bowl, mix Dream Whip, cream cheese, crushed pineapple, and coconut. Let chill for 30 minutes. Add to cracker mixture and serve.

Taco Salad

1 pound ground beef, chuck, or sirloin
1 medium onion, chopped
1 16-ounce can light kidney beans
2 medium tomatoes, chopped
1 10-ounce bag taco, nachos, or Tostidos chips
1 12-ounce package shredded cheddar cheese
1 medium head iceberg lettuce
1 10-ounce jar taco sauce, optional
  sour cream, optional

Fry hamburger for 15 minutes on medium heat or until done. Drain kidney beans; put in hamburger. Cook until warm. In a large bowl, tear lettuce into medium-sized pieces. Top lettuce with tomatoes, onions, and crumbled chips. After draining hamburger & bean mixture, pour on top of lettuce while hot. Top with the shredded cheddar cheese. Serve immediately.

Servings: 4-6

Sides: sour cream and taco sauce

Tip: Hit the bottom of iceberg lettuce on a hard surface to de-stem it.

CHAPTER 3

Casseroles

*The Stevens and Knight families
enjoying their Sunday dinner together.*

Cookin' Notes

Chicken Casserole

1 small chicken, cooked and deboned (3-5 pounds)
2 10¾-ounce cans cream of celery soup
¼ cup milk
½ teaspoon Worcestershire sauce
1 6-ounce can mushrooms
1 8-ounce bag stuffing mix

Cook whole chicken in a large pot of water for 50 minutes. Debone chicken & cut into pieces. Place in bottom of 9x13 casserole dish. Mix soup, milk, Worcestershire sauce, and mushrooms in small bowl; pour over chicken. Fix stuffing according to directions; spread on top of chicken mixture. Bake at 350 degrees for 25 minutes or until hot & bubbly.

History: In 1838, Lea & Perrins bought the Worcestershire sauce recipe.

Mexican Cornbread Casserole

     2   pounds ground beef
   1½   cups onion, chopped
     3   6-ounce packages Jiffy Cornbread Mix
     1   14.75-ounce can cream-style corn
     1   8-ounce package shredded cheddar cheese
     1   12-ounce bottle picante sauce
     1   10-ounce bottle taco sauce
         sour cream (optional)

Brown beef and onion. Drain the grease. In large bowl, prepare cornbread mixture according to instructions; add creamed corn. Preheat oven to 400 degrees. Grease a 9x13 casserole dish. Pour ½ of cream corn/cornbread mixture on bottom of casserole dish. Top with beef and onion mixture. Pour picante sauce evenly over top. Pour taco sauce on top then sprinkle with cheddar cheese. Pour the remaining cream corn/ cornbread mixture on top. Lower oven temperature to 375 degrees and bake until golden brown (about 1 hour). Serve hot.

Accompaniment: dollop of sour cream on individual servings

Tip: To stop the burning sensation from spicy food, drink cold milk.

Beef & Cheese Upside-Down Cornbread Casserole

2	tablespoons butter
1½	pounds ground beef
1	6-ounce can tomato paste
1	teaspoon chili powder
1	cup cubed cheddar cheese
½	cup green olives, sliced
1	cup onions, chopped
1	tablespoon flour
1/8	teaspoon pepper
1	8.5-ounce box Jiffy Cornbread Mix

In a large skillet, melt butter. Add beef and onions. Cook until beef is lightly browned. Stir in flour; add tomato paste, salt, chili powder, and pepper. Remove from heat. Add cheese & olives. Spread evenly over the bottom of a 9x9x2 inch baking dish. Prepare muffin mix according to directions on package. Spread over beef mixture. Bake in a preheated 400 degrees oven for 30-40 minutes. Let stand for 5 minutes in the pan. Loosen around edges & invert onto platter. Serve hot.

Servings: 6

History: The Forme of Cury, *written in 1390 by Eliza Acton Born, is the oldest surviving English cookbook.*

Sausage Casserole

12 slices white bread (decrusted and cubed)
 1 pound grated sharp cheddar cheese
 2 pounds sausage, browned
 1 4-ounce can dried chilies
 4 eggs
2½ cups cold milk
 1 tablespoon mustard
   salt and pepper to taste
 1 10¾-ounce can cream of mushroom soup
1/3 cup cold milk

Place bread crumbs in 13x9 casserole dish. Layer sausage, chilies, and cheese. Mix eggs, milk, mustard, and salt and pepper. Pour over sausage mixture. Refrigerate overnight. Before baking, mix cream of mushroom soup with cold milk. Pour evenly over casserole. Bake at 300 degrees for 1½ hours.

Serves: 15-20 or divide in half to serve 10.

History: Sliced bread was introduced in 1928.

Hash Brown Casserole

2   16-ounce bags frozen hash browns (do not thaw)

1   8-ounce carton sour cream

1   10¾-ounce can cream of chicken soup

1   10-ounce shredded sharp cheddar cheese

½   cup chopped onions

1   teaspoon salt

1   teaspoon pepper

1   stick butter

    corn flakes or potato chips

    salt and pepper to taste

Mix first 5 ingredients together; pour into 9x13 casserole dish. Add salt and pepper. Cover evenly with corn flakes. Pour melted stick of butter on top of corn flakes. Bake at 375 degrees for 45 minutes.

Note: May need to add more cheese, if desired.

Summer Squash Casserole

  1   pound yellow summer squash sliced (about 3 cups)

1/8   cup chopped onions

  ½   can cream of mushroom soup

  ½   cup sour cream

  ½   cup shredded carrot

  ½   8-ounce package herb-seasoned stuffing mix

  ¼   cup melted butter

  1   tablespoon salt

Cook squash and onion in boiling water (salted) for 5 minutes; drain.
Combine soup and sour cream. Stir in shredded carrot. Blend in the
squash and onion. In a separate bowl, combine stuffing and butter.
Spread ½ of stuffing mixture in bottom of a medium-sized casserole
dish. Spoon in vegetable mixture over stuffing. Cover the vegetables
with remaining stuffing mix. Bake at 350 degrees for 25-30 minutes.
Serve hot.

Serves: 3-5 persons

Tip: Bake food in a glass casserole dish at 325 degrees or it may burn.

Jean's Squash Casserole

2   cups cooked squash

¾   stick butter

2   eggs

1   teaspoon salt

½   teaspoon pepper

1   cup onions, chopped

1   cup shredded cheddar cheese

1   cup evaporated milk

2   cups stuffing mix (8-ounce bag)

¼   teaspoon thyme

Mix all ingredients in large bowl; pour into greased casserole dish. Bake at 375 degrees for approximately 40 minutes.

Broccoli Casserole

1   cup onions, chopped

1   cup celery, chopped

2   16-ounce packages chopped broccoli (thawed)

8   ounces Cheese Whiz

1¾   cans cream of mushroom soup

   (Note: you may want to add ¼ can of soup leftover if you think
   more moisture is needed)

2   cups cooked rice

1   stick butter

Prep: Chop onions, celery, and cook rice.

Sauté chopped onions and celery in 1 stick of butter for 20 minutes.
Mix chopped broccoli, Cheese Whiz, and mushroom soup in a casserole
dish. Add onions/celery mixture and 2 cups of cooked rice. Mix all
ingredients thoroughly. Bake uncovered in the oven for 1 hour at 350
degrees. Serve hot.

*History: Cheese Whiz was introduced in 1953 as a shortcut for
   homemakers.*

Spinach Casserole

1   medium onion, chopped

1/2   8-ounce package cream cheese (softened)

1   16-ounce package frozen chopped spinach

1   egg, beaten

¼   cup bread crumbs

   salt and pepper to taste

Preheat oven to 350 degrees. Mix all ingredients; pour into buttered
casserole dish. Bake uncovered for 20 minutes.

*History: Spinach was the first frozen vegetable to be sold. In 1937,
   United States spinach growers erected a statue in honor of Popeye the
   Sailor Man, a favorite cartoon character.*

Cauliflower Casserole

1	head cauliflower
1	cup mushrooms (2 4-ounce cans)
¼	cup green peppers, diced
¼	cup sweet red peppers, diced
¼	cup melted butter
1/3	cup all-purpose flour
2	cups milk
1	teaspoon salt
1	cup shredded Swiss cheese

Prep: Chop green and red peppers. Cut cauliflower head into pieces.

Cook cauliflower in boiling water for 8-10 minutes. Drain. Sauté mushrooms, green peppers, and red peppers in butter until tender. Add flour. Cook for 1 minute, stirring constantly. Gradually, add milk and remove from heat. Add salt and cheese; stir until cheese melts. In buttered casserole dish, alternate layers of cauliflower/cheese sauce. Bake at 325 degrees for 15 minutes. Garnish with parsley or red pepper strips.

Tip: Spray oven cleaner on burnt food in a glass casserole dish and let it soak for 30 minutes.

Eggplant Casserole

1   large eggplant

1   cup onions, chopped

1   cup tomato soup

1   cup cracker crumbs

1   egg

1   tablespoon butter

   grated Parmesan cheese

Prep: Chop eggplant and onion.

Boil eggplant and onion until well-done and soft. Drain; mash thoroughly. Mix other ingredients; put in buttered casserole dish. Add more cracker crumbs, cheese, and melted butter on top. Bake at 350 degrees for 30 minutes.

History: In 1932, Campbell's invented the tomato soup.

Zucchini Casserole

1   pound hamburger

¼   cup onion, chopped

1/3 cup green pepper, chopped

3   cups zucchini, sliced

5-6 tomatoes, sliced

¾   cup water

½   teaspoon salt

1   cup angel hair spaghetti

Brown hamburger using olive oil (do not pour out grease). Add vegetables and water; simmer for 10 minutes. Cook angel hair spaghetti for 3-4 minutes in boiling, salted water; drain. Layer vegetables, meat, and spaghetti in a 2-quart casserole dish. Bake at 350 degrees for 45 minutes.

Tip: Tomatoes should always be kept at room temperature before slicing. The taste of a tomato changes if chilled in the refrigerator.

Vegetarian Zucchini Casserole

In a large casserole dish, layer the following ingredients in order:

½	stick butter, melted
	zucchini, sliced
	onions, diced
	green peppers, chopped
4	medium potatoes, sliced
	Romano cheese
	zucchini, sliced
	Romano cheese
	mozzarella cheese

Dribble top of dish with 1 tablespoon olive oil. Bake at 375 degrees for 1 hour.

Tips: In certain areas, green peppers were also known as mangoes. Green peppers can be refrigerated for 1 week or frozen up to 6 months.

Lucille's Sweet Potato Casserole

2	pounds sweet potatoes boiled, peeled and mashed
2	eggs, beaten
2	tablespoons butter, melted
½	cup brown sugar
¼	teaspoon baking soda
½	teaspoon nutmeg
½	teaspoon cinnamon

Preheat oven to 350 degrees. Combine all ingredients; mix well. Pour into a casserole dish. Mixture may be very soupy; will thicken when baked. Bake at 350 degrees for 1 hour.

Note: Cinnamon is one of the first known spices. It helps to boost your metabolism.

Fourth of July Bean Casserole

½ pound sliced and diced bacon

1 cup onions, chopped

1 16-ounce can lima or butter beans, drained

½ cup ketchup

½ cup packed brown sugar

2 tablespoons molasses

½ teaspoon chili powder

1 16-ounce can kidney beans, drained

½ pound ground beef

1 28-ounce can pork and beans

½ cup barbecue sauce (may use recipe in cookbook)

½ cup sugar

2 tablespoons yellow mustard

1 teaspoon salt

In a large skillet, cook bacon, beef, and onion until meat is browned and onion is tender. Drain. Transfer to a greased 2½ quart casserole dish; add all beans and mix well. In a small bowl, combine all remaining ingredients. Pour over beef and bean mixture; stir well. Cover and bake at 350 degrees for 45 minutes. Uncover; bake an additional 15 minutes.

Note: January 6th has been designated as National Bean Day.

CHAPTER 4

Main Dishes

Great-grandfather Lewis bringing home dinner.

Cookin' Notes

Lasagna

2   pounds ground chuck or ground sirloin

1   large onion, diced

1   jar spaghetti sauce (1 lb. 10-ounce jar)

2   7-ounce cans mushrooms

1   24-ounce container cottage cheese (large curd)

1   8-ounce package shredded mozzarella cheese

1   8-ounce container sour cream

1   pound box lasagna noodles (will not use all of the noodles)
    salt & pepper to taste
    grated Parmesan cheese (optional)

In a pan, fry ground chuck and diced onions together. Drain grease. In a large pot, combine beef/onion mixture, spaghetti sauce, mushrooms, and salt/pepper to taste. Heat for 10 minutes. In a large pot of boiling water, add 1 pound box of lasagna noodles. Add 2 tablespoons of oil to water to keep noodles from sticking together. Boil 8-9 minutes, stirring frequently. Drain & let cool in colander. In a 9 x 13 casserole dish, put 1 layer of lasagna noodles. Spread a light cover of sour cream over the noodles. Put ½ of the spaghetti sauce over noodles. Spread ½ container of cottage cheese over sauce. Sprinkle ½ package of shredded mozzarella cheese on top of cottage cheese. Put 2nd layer of lasagna noodles on top of mozzarella cheese and repeat the same procedure. Cover dish with foil. Bake in oven 350 degrees for 70 minutes. After removing from oven, let stand for approximately 10 minutes. Cut into serving pieces.

Yields: 10-12 servings

Suggestion: Top individual servings with grated Parmesan cheese (optional).

Note: Can use extra noodles to make ricotta lasagna rollups.

Swiss Chicken Delight

4-6   chicken breasts, boneless & skinless

4-6   Swiss cheese slices

1   10.5-ounce can cream of chicken soup

6   ounces water

½   cup butter, melted

2   cups herb seasoned stuffing mix (8-ounce package)

Place chicken in a single layer in baking dish. Top each breast with a slice of Swiss cheese. Mix soup and water together and pour over chicken breasts. Mix stuffing mix and butter then sprinkle over chicken. Cover with foil; bake at 325 degrees for 1½ hours. Serve hot.

Servings: 4-6

Cheesy Broccoli Chicken Roll-Ups

1   10-ounce package frozen broccoli spears

6   chicken breast halves, boneless & skinless

4   ounces cheddar or Swiss cheese, cut into 6 strips

1   10.5-ounce can broccoli cheese soup

6   ounces water

½   teaspoon mustard, Dijon style

Cook broccoli in boiling water for 10 minutes. Drain. Place broccoli spear and cheese strip in the center of each breast half; roll up. Place chicken rolls seam down in 12 x 8 inch baking dish. Combine remaining ingredients; pour over chicken rolls. Bake at 375 degrees for 35 minutes. Test doneness of chicken with a fork.

History: In 1928, broccoli is introduced in the United States.

Chicken Vegetable Sauté

cooking spray

4 chicken breast halves, skinless & boneless

8 ounces chopped broccoli

1 4-ounce can sliced mushrooms

1 medium carrot, thinly sliced

1 10¾-ounce can cream of broccoli soup

¾ cup milk

¼ teaspoon dried thyme

Spray skillet with cooking spray. Heat over medium-high heat for 1 minute. Add chicken breasts; cook 10 minutes or until browned on both sides. Remove; set aside. Remove chicken from skillet. Reduce heat to medium and spray skillet again with cooking spray. Add vegetables; cook until tender. Stir frequently. Add soup, milk, and thyme. Boil mixture. Return chicken to skillet. Reduce to low heat. Cover and cook for 5 minutes or until chicken is no longer pink; stirring occasionally.

Servings: 4

Tip: Covering chicken after it has been fried will cause it to lose its crispiness.

Chicken Pot Pie

12	ounces chicken
1	15-ounce can mixed vegetables
1	10¾-ounce can cream of chicken soup
½	cup milk
1/3	cup water
2	9-inch pie shells

Mix ingredients together in a bowl. Pour mixture into pie shell. Remove other pie shell from tin pan and layer over the top. Press edges of crust together to seal. Bake in 450 degrees oven for 30 minutes.

Serves: 4

Suggestion: Turkey or beef could be used instead of chicken.

Picnic Chicken

1	egg
2	tablespoons milk
1	1.5-ounce package spaghetti sauce mix
¼	cup flour
3	tablespoons grated Parmesan cheese
1	frying chicken, cut up
	oil for frying

Whisk egg and milk in a bowl. Mix thoroughly the spaghetti sauce mix, flour, and cheese. Dip chicken pieces in egg mixture and then spaghetti sauce mixture. Fry in hot oil in a large skillet for 25 minutes, turning to brown evenly. Cover with foil and cook 25 minutes longer until tender. Chill. Serve cold.

Servings: 4

Tip: To prevent splashing when frying meat, sprinkle a pinch of salt into the pan.

Dixie Barbecued Chicken

1	cup ketchup
2½	tablespoons honey
1	tablespoon bottled lemon juice
¼	teaspoon hot pepper sauce
2-3	pounds frying chicken, cut up
	salt and pepper to taste

Combine ketchup, honey, lemon juice and hot sauce. Set aside. Bake chicken at 375 degrees for one hour or until the juices run clear. If grilling, grill chicken 6-7 minutes per side. Turn once to cook evenly on both sides. Brush the ketchup mixture on chicken & continue to bake or grill for 10 minutes. Let rest 5 minutes before serving.

Servings: 4-5

Suggestion: May want to use Barbecue Sauce recipe in this cookbook.

Note: 100 crops in the United States depend on honeybees for pollination.

Chicken a la King

4 tablespoons butter

1 4-ounce can sliced mushrooms

½ green or red pepper, chopped

2 tablespoons butter

2 tablespoons flour

4 ounces milk and 4-ounces chicken broth, combined

   salt & pepper to taste

1 egg

2-3 tablespoons cream

8-12 ounces cooked chicken

Add 4 tablespoons of butter in a pan on low heat. Add mushroom slices and chopped pepper. Cook until tender. Set aside. In a pot, mix 2 tablespoons of butter, flour, milk/broth mixture, salt and pepper. Mix thoroughly. When sauce is thick, add the egg and cream; blend together. Cook gently without boiling for 2-3 minutes. Add mushroom slices and chopped pepper. Simmer. Coarsely chop the chicken; add to the pot. Heat for 2 minutes. Put 2 pieces of toast on each dish and cover with chicken mixture. Serve immediately.

Servings: 4

Suggestion: May serve on cooked rice instead of toast.

Chicken Fettuccine Alfredo

4   cups cubed cooked chicken

1   pint whipping cream

¾   cup grated Parmesan cheese

1   teaspoon black pepper

4   egg yolks

1   12-ounce pkg. broad egg noodles, cooked

In a pan, heat cream to warm. Add Parmesan cheese and black pepper. Whisk in egg yolks. Add cubed chicken to mixture. If too thick, add a small amount of milk. Continue to heat until warm. Cook egg noodles according to directions on package; drain. Pour chicken mixture over cooked noodles. Serve hot.

Serves: 6-8

Tip: Put 2 tablespoons of butter or oil in the water when cooking rice, beans, or pasta to keep them from boiling over the pot.

Chicken Cacciatore

    1   pound boneless chicken strips
    ½   cup chopped onion
    1   minced garlic clove
    2   tablespoons oil
    1   28-ounce can diced tomatoes
    1   8-ounce can tomato sauce
    1   teaspoon salt
    ½   teaspoon oregano
    ½   teaspoon basil
  1/8   teaspoon red pepper flakes
    1   cup green pepper strips
   1½   cups cooked rice

Brown chicken, onion and garlic in oil for 20 minutes or until golden brown. Add tomatoes, tomato sauce, seasonings, and green pepper. Bring to a boil. Stir in cooked rice. Cover; remove from heat. Let stand for 5 minutes. Stir before serving.

Servings: 4

Suggestion: Substitute 1 16-ounce jar spaghetti sauce instead of using garlic, diced tomatoes, tomato sauce, salt, and red pepper.

Party Chicken

8 large chicken breasts, skinless & boneless

8 slices bacon

1 4.5-ounce jar chipped beef

1 10¾-ounce can cream of mushroom soup

2 cups sour cream

Wrap each piece of bacon around chicken breast. Put in 9x13 baking dish. Arrange chipped beef on top of chicken breasts. Mix sour cream and mushroom soup together; pour over top of chicken & chipped beef. Bake at 250 degrees for 3 hours.

Tip: Roll a package of bacon into a tube before opening. This will loosen the slices & keep them from sticking together.

Chicken & Dumplings

4 large chicken breasts with skins
  water
3 14-ounce cans chicken broth
  salt & pepper to taste
1 32-ounce box Bisquick
2 cups milk

Step 1. Place chicken breasts in an 8 quart pot and cover with water. Boil chicken breasts in water for approximately 50 minutes. Remove breasts. Let cool in a bowl before removing skins & deboning meat. Set boiled water aside for later.

Step 2. Remove skins & debone chicken. Tear into medium-sized pieces.

Step 3. In a bowl, add Bisquick and milk. Mix thoroughly. Set aside.

Step 4. Add chicken broth to water and bring to a boil. Add salt and pepper to mixture.

Step 5. Drop dumpling mixture into boiling broth/water by using a tablespoon. Cook dumplings for 20 minutes on medium-high heat. Stir mixture carefully to avoid breaking dumplings into pieces.

Step 6. Add chicken pieces to pot. Stir carefully. Cook for 10 minutes.

Serves: 6-8

Accompaniments: mashed potatoes and green beans

Chicken Spaghetti

2 chicken fryers, 2-3 pounds each

3 celery stalks, cut ½" slices

1 green pepper, chopped

¼ teaspoon garlic powder

1 4-ounce can sliced mushrooms

1 16-ounce can diced tomatoes

1 10¾-ounce can cream of mushroom soup

½ teaspoon salt, black pepper, paprika

¼ teaspoon Worcestershire sauce

1 pound Velveeta cheese, cubed

2 tablespoons green or black olives, chopped (optional)

1 pound box spaghetti

In large pot, put chicken and cover with water. Boil chicken for 45 minutes or until tender. Remove chicken and let cool. Reserve 1 quart of the broth. Remove skins and debone chicken. Tear into bite-size pieces. Put pieces in a bowl and set aside. Put celery, green pepper, onions, garlic powder, and mushrooms into reserved broth and cook for 10 minutes. Add spaghetti; cook for 9 minutes. Add remaining ingredients and chicken pieces; mixing thoroughly. Cook over low heat until cheese is melted. Serve hot.

Servings: 10-12

Country Fried Steak with Gravy

1   pound ground steak

1   teaspoon salt

¼   cup flour

½   cup cold water or milk

     salt & pepper

     oil for frying

Cut meat in serving pieces. Salt and pepper meat to liking. Roll in flour. Put oil in an iron skillet and add the steak pieces when oil is hot. Cook meat for 10 minutes or until done. Add water and reduce heat. Simmer until meat is tender. Remove meat from pan. Add 1 tablespoon flour and water or milk to drippings in pan to make gravy. Serve gravy as a side or on top of steak.

Tip: Brown gravy in a hurry with a bit of instant coffee straight from the jar. There is no bitter taste.

Stuffed Steak Rolls

2   pounds round steak ½" thick

3   slices bacon

1/3   cup chopped onions

¼   cup chopped celery

2   cups bread crumbs

2   teaspoons parsley flakes

1   egg, beaten

½   cup flour

1   teaspoon poultry seasoning

¼   teaspoon salt

¼   teaspoon sage

¼   teaspoon pepper

¼   cup oil

1   10-ounce can beef broth

1   bay leaf

Pound meat to 1/8 inch thickness and cut each into 6 pieces. Set aside. Fry bacon in a large skillet until crisp. Remove from skillet; crumble & set aside. Reserve 2 tablespoons drippings in skillet. Add onions & celery to skillet; sauté until tender. In a bowl, combine crumbled bacon, sautéed vegetables, bread crumbs, parsley & egg. Mix well. Place 1 heaping tablespoon of stuffing on each piece of steak. Roll up each piece & secure with wooden toothpicks. Set aside. Combine flour, poultry seasoning, salt, sage, and pepper together. Dredge each steak roll in the flour mixture & brown in hot oil in a large skillet. Transfer steak rolls to a casserole dish. Add beef broth & bay leaf. Cover and bake at 375 degrees for 1 hour. Remove bay leaf before serving.

Yield: 6 servings

Suggestion: Save extra bread crumbs and add to scrambled eggs. Bread crumbs will improve the flavor & certainly help make larger portions.

Cubed Steaks with an Italian Twist

½ cup flour

½ teaspoon salt & pepper

1 teaspoon paprika & oregano

¼ teaspoon curry

¼ cup oil

4 ounces mozzarella cheese

1 14-ounce jar pizza sauce

6 cube steaks (or bucket steak)

Mix flour & spices in a bowl. Rub steaks with mixture. Brown meat in oil & remove to a baking dish. Top steaks with pizza sauce & mozzarella cheese. Bake for 20 minutes at 325 degrees. Serve hot.

For testing purposes: Ragu Pizza Sauce was used. Homemade sauce would be an excellent substitute.

Easy Beef Stroganoff

1   pound sirloin or tenderloin

1   tablespoon oil or 2 tablespoons butter

1   10¾-ounce can cream of mushroom soup

1   cup sour cream

1   small onion, chopped

1   garlic clove, crushed (optional)

1   tablespoon parsley

¼   cup tomato juice

1   4-ounce can sliced mushrooms

1   12-ounce package egg noodles or 3 cups cooked rice

Cook meat in oil or butter for 4½ minutes until pinkness is gone. Remove meat from pan. Add onions and mushrooms to pan; cook until tender, approximately 8 minutes. Mix soup and sour cream together. Place mixture and cooked meat in pan and heat thoroughly (do not boil). Serve over hot egg noodles or rice and chopped parsley.

History: In 1848, pasta was produced commercially in the United States.

Tip: For perfect noodles, bring required amount of water to a boil, add noodles, turn off heat & allow to stand for 20 minutes.

Shoemaker's Beef

1½ pounds round steak
 1 package Lipton's French Onion or Onion/Mushroom Mix
 1 10¾-ounce can cream of mushroom soup
 ½ cup water

Cook in crock pot on low heat for 8 hours. Serve over hot egg noodles.

Servings: 4

History: In 1952, Lipton Soup Company dehydrated onion soup mix.

Salisbury Steak with Mushroom-Onion Gravy

- 1 envelope onion soup mix
- 2 cups water
- 1½ pounds ground beef
- ¼ cup chopped parsley
- ¼ cup all-purpose flour
- 1½ tablespoons butter
- 1 large onion, sliced
- 12 ounces fresh mushrooms, thinly sliced
- 1 beef bouillon cube

Mix 2 tablespoons of the soup mix and ¼ cup of the water in a large bowl. Add beef and parsley. Mix until blended. Shape into four oval patties. Coat patties with 1½ tablespoons of flour. Melt butter in a large skillet over medium heat. Add patties and cook about 10 minutes, turning once, until crusty and no longer pink in the middle. Remove to a plate and cover to keep warm. Add onion, mushrooms, and ¼ cup water to dripping in skillet. Stir with wooden spoon to scrape up any brown bits on bottom. Reduce heat to medium-low, cover and cook for 10 minutes. Mix remaining soup mix, 1½ cups water and 2½ tablespoons flour in a small bowl. Stir into mushroom mixture, add bouillon cube and bring to a boil. Cook until thickened, about 3 minutes. Stir frequently. Return patties to skillet and turn to coat with gravy. Remove to plates or a platter. Serve with remaining gravy.

Servings: 4

Tip: Thicken gravy with milk or broth blended with flour.

Joy's Meatloaf

3   pounds ground beef, chuck, or sirloin

1   medium onion, diced

3   eggs

8   slices bread, crumbled

1   15-ounce can tomato sauce (9 oz. for meat & 6 oz. for top)

½   cup milk

1   1.5-ounce package meat loaf seasoning

    salt & pepper to taste

Mix all ingredients together. Makes 2 medium-sized loaves or 1 large loaf. Bake 375 degrees for 1½ hours or until thoroughly cooked. Brush the topping on loaves the last 20 minutes of baking.

Tip: Mix ingredients with a potato masher to avoid getting mixture on hands.

Topping for Meatloaf

6   ounces tomato sauce

¼   cup ketchup

1   teaspoon mustard

2   tablespoons maple syrup

Mix all ingredients together and brush on meat the last 20 minutes of the baking cycle.

Servings: 10-12 (ingredients may be halved for a smaller loaf)

Note: Will need to drain liquid from meat twice during the cooking cycle.

Pepper Steak

 2 pounds round steak, cut into strips
 3 tablespoons oil
 2 cups water
 1 15-ounce can stewed tomatoes
 2 beef bouillon cubes
 2 green peppers, cut into strips
 2 tablespoons soy sauce
 3 tablespoons cornstarch
 2 4-ounce cans sliced mushrooms
 ½ cup water
 1 12-ounce package egg noodles or 3 cups rice, cooked

Brown meat in oil. Stirring, add 2 cups water, tomatoes, and bouillon cubes. Bring to a boil. Cover. Simmer for 1 hour. Add pepper strips and mushrooms. Simmer 20-30 minutes. Blend cornstarch, soy sauce, and ½ cup water in a bowl. Add to meat. Mix until thick. Serve hot over cooked rice or egg noodles.

Stuffed Green Peppers

6-8 green peppers

2 pounds hamburger

½ cup celery, diced

1 15-ounce can tomato sauce

1 large can (1 pound 12-ounce) diced tomatoes

1 medium onion, diced

½ cup ketchup

1½ cups cooked rice

     salt & pepper to taste

Cut tops off the green peppers. Hollow out the insides of the peppers. Wash and put in a large pot. Cover with water. Boil for 15-20 minutes. Remove peppers and drain on paper towels. In a large bowl, mix hamburger, celery, onion, ketchup, cooked rice, and salt & pepper to taste. Stuff peppers with hamburger mixture. Place in baking dish. Mix tomato sauce and diced tomatoes then pour evenly over the peppers. Bake in 350 degrees oven for 45 minutes. Serve hot.

Serves: 6-8

Suggestion: Can use 1 pound fried, crumbled sausage instead of hamburger.

Tip: Green peppers can be diced, cubed, or cut in strips and frozen for later usage.

Note: A muffin pan is an excellent pan to use when baking stuffed green peppers.

Beef Stew

2½	pounds beef cubes
3	medium carrots, cut into ½" slices
1	stalk celery, cut into ½" slices
1	medium onion, chopped
2	medium potatoes, cubed
1	28-ounce can whole tomatoes
32	ounces beef stock or 2 cans beef broth
1	clove garlic, minced
	salt & pepper to taste
	Roux (below)

Brown beef cubes in a frying pan on low heat. Add beef cubes and the remaining ingredients, except roux, in a medium-sized pot. Simmer for 1-1½ hours. Add roux to thicken as desired the last 30 minutes of cooking.

Yields: 1 gallon

Roux

Combine equal parts of flour and melted butter (usually 4 tablespoons each ingredient). Put in a small skillet. Stir the mixture over low heat until smooth.

Leftover Tip: Half a loaf of crusty bread (approx. 1½ pounds). Scoop out insides of each half. Fill bread halves with the stew.

Heavenly Swiss Steak

    1   4 pound roast
    ¼   cup flour
    ½   teaspoon salt and pepper
    ¼   teaspoon garlic powder
  2-3   tablespoons oil
    1   16-ounce can diced tomatoes
    1   medium onion, sliced
    1   small green pepper, sliced
    ¼   cup water, if needed

Heat oil in large skillet. Season roast with salt, pepper, and garlic powder. Dredge in flour; brown on both sides in hot oil. Place in roasting pan. Put onion and pepper slices on top of roast. Pour diced tomatoes over top of vegetables. Cover and bake at 300 degrees for 3½ hours. Check roast in oven on an hourly basis to see if water is needed. If so, add ¼ cup of water to the pan.

Servings: 6

Suggestion: Serve with mashed potatoes since this recipe makes it own gravy.

Hamburger Stroganoff

1   pound ground beef, chuck, or sirloin

½   cup chopped onion

4   tablespoons butter

2   tablespoons flour

1   teaspoon garlic salt

¼   teaspoon black pepper

1   6-ounce can mushroom pieces, drained

1   10¾-ounce can cream of chicken

1   cup sour cream

1   12-ounce package egg noodles

Cook meat and chopped onion in a skillet for 20 minutes. Stir in flour, garlic salt, pepper, and mushrooms; cook for 5 minutes. Stir in soup; heat to boiling, stirring frequently. Reduce heat; simmer uncovered for 10 minutes. Stir in sour cream and mix thoroughly. Boil egg noodles according to directions on the package; drain. Serve meat mixture over noodles. Serve hot.

Beef Stroganoff

1½ pounds round steak, cut into strips

½ cup onions, chopped

1 10¾-ounce can tomato soup

1 cup sour cream

¼ cup butter

1 6-ounce can mushrooms, sliced

1 garlic clove, minced

salt & pepper to taste

Brown beef strips in butter for 10 minutes or until brown. Add mushrooms, onions, and garlic. Cook another 10 minutes or until onions are translucent. Blend in soup, sour cream, salt, and pepper. Cover and simmer about 1 hour or until meat is tender. Stir occasionally. Serve hot.

Yields: 4-5 servings

Suggestion: Serve over cooked egg noodles or cooked rice.

Pot Roast

3-4   pound chuck roast or rump pot roast

¼   cup flour

½   cup water

1   tablespoon dill seed

2   medium onions, sliced

2   tablespoons oil

salt & black pepper to taste

Roll roast in flour. Put oil in large skillet or Dutch oven pan. Heat roast in hot oil. Brown meat on both sides. Season meat with dill seed, salt, and pepper. Place sliced onions on top of meat. Add ½ cup water. Cover and simmer for 2-3 hours or until meat is tender.

Servings: 6-8

Tip: It is necessary to let a beef, pork, lamb, or poultry sit awhile before cutting. It allows the juices to retreat back into the meat. If it is cut too soon, the juices will spill onto the platter.

Claudia's Steak San Marco

2   lbs. chuck steak, cut into bite-size pieces

1   envelope Lipton Onion Soup Mix

1   16-ounce can Italian peeled tomatoes

1   teaspoon oregano

2   tablespoons vegetable oil

2   tablespoons wine vinegar

1   6-ounce can mushrooms

1/8   teaspoon black pepper

1/8   teaspoon garlic powder

Add cooking oil to large skillet. Cut meat into bite size-pieces; add to skillet. Brown meat on low heat. Drain liquid. Add remaining ingredients. Cover with lid or foil. Simmer for 1 hour or until meat is tender.

Serves: 4

Suggestion: Serve on mashed potatoes, rice, or noodles.

Delicious Hot Dog Sauce

2½ pounds ground beef or chuck

2¼ cups finely chopped onions

  3 cups water

  1 24-ounce bottle ketchup

  1 pint tomato juice

1¼ teaspoons chili powder

1/8 cup brown sugar

1½ tablespoons white vinegar

  ¾ teaspoon black pepper

  1 teaspoon Tabasco sauce (or any hot sauce)

  1 teaspoon Worcestershire sauce

     salt to taste

Bring water, onions, and beef to boil for 10 minutes in a large pot. Simmer for 40 minutes, stirring occasionally. Drain water. Mix other ingredients in mixture and simmer for 2 hours.

Yields: 5 pounds (May reduce ingredients if only fixing one meal)

Suggestion: This sauce recipe is excellent to freeze for later usage. After sauce is cooled, fill quart-size freezer bags ½ to ¾ full. Easy to thaw & heat when needed.

For testing purposes: Heinz ketchup & Tabasco sauce were used in the recipe.

Spaghetti Sauce

1   pound ground beef, chuck, or sirloin
2   tablespoons oil for frying
2   medium onions, chopped
2   teaspoons chili powder
¼   teaspoon oregano
1   teaspoon sugar
1   teaspoon salt
¼   teaspoon black pepper
¼   cup ketchup
½   teaspoon Worcestershire sauce
1   6-ounce can tomato puree
1   14.5-ounce can diced tomatoes
1   cup water
½   cup Parmesan cheese

Add 2 tablespoons oil to large pot. Cook meat for 10 minutes on medium heat or until done; stirring on a regular basis. Add onions in meat mixture and sauté for 10 minutes. Drain liquids before adding the other ingredients, excluding the Parmesan cheese. Simmer sauce for approximately 1½-2 hours. Before serving, add Parmesan cheese and mix thoroughly. Serve hot over cooked spaghetti noodles.

Serving: 4-6

Tip: Pour sauce over elbow macaroni shells and call it "Goulash."

Mark's Italian Delight Spaghetti Sauce

1   pound ground beef, chuck, or sirloin
1   28-ounce can diced tomatoes
1   15-ounce can tomato sauce
1   1.5-ounce package spaghetti mix
1   7.3-ounce jar button mushrooms
1   medium onion, diced
1   teaspoon dried minced onions
½   teaspoon prepared chopped garlic (in a jar)
½   garlic clove, chopped
½   teaspoon salt & black pepper
¼   teaspoon red pepper
1/8   cup sugar
½   cup Parmesan cheese

In a large pot, boil beef and onions in water for 20 minutes. Drain water. Combine the other ingredients in pot, excluding Parmesan cheese. Simmer sauce mixture for 40 minutes, stirring occasionally. Last 5 minutes of cooking, add Parmesan cheese. Mix thoroughly. Serve hot over cooked linguini or angel hair pasta.

Servings: 6-8

Accompaniments: cole slaw or garden salad; garlic, Italian, or rye bread

Manicotti

These noodles can be stuffed with a cheese or meat mixture

Cheese Filling

- 1 16-ounce carton ricotta cheese or small curd cottage cheese
- 2 cups mozzarella cheese
- 3 eggs, beaten
- ¾ cup grated Parmesan cheese
- 1 tablespoon parsley flakes
- ½ cup bread crumbs
  salt & pepper to taste

- 1 box manicotti noodles; cook as directed on box (drain thoroughly)
- 1 jar favorite spaghetti sauce or use recipe in cookbook

Combine 1 cup of mozzarella cheese and the other 5 ingredients together in a large bowl. Add salt and pepper to taste. Stuff manicotti noodles. Put a layer of sauce on the bottom of baking dish. Add stuffed manicotti in a single layer. Pour remaining sauce over the top. Sprinkle 1 cup of mozzarella cheese over sauce. Cover with foil and bake at 350 degrees for 30 minutes. Uncover and cook for 15 minutes longer. Serve hot.

Meat Filling

- 1 pound sausage, mild or hot
- 2 15-ounce cans tomato sauce
- 1 6-ounce can tomato paste
- ¼ cup water
- 1 egg
- ½ cup grated Parmesan cheese
- 1 15-ounce ricotta cheese
- 3 cups mozzarella cheese
- 1 teaspoon parsley flakes

In a large sauce pan, brown sausage; drain. Remove ½ of the sausage and set aside. Stir in tomato sauce, paste, water, and brown sugar into the sausage. Simmer 15 minutes. In medium bowl, combine remaining sausage, ricotta cheese, 2 cups mozzarella cheese, egg, and parsley. In 13x9x2 dish, pour 1/3 of the sauce. Stuff noodles with ricotta mixture and place on sauce in a single layer. Pour rest of sauce over filled noodles. Top with remaining mozzarella cheese; sprinkle with Parmesan cheese. Bake uncovered at 350 degrees for 20-25 minutes.

Quote: George Bernard Shaw said, "There is no love sincerer than the love of food."

Mark's Spaghetti Meatballs

6	slices white bread
1½	pounds ground beef, chuck, or sirloin
½	cup oats
1	teaspoon garlic powder
1	small onion, chopped
½	teaspoon red and black pepper
1	teaspoon salt
½	cup Parmesan cheese

Combine all ingredients in a large bowl. Mix thoroughly and form into 1" inch balls. Fry in skillet on low heat for 20 minutes or until done. Constantly turn meatballs so browning occurs on all sides.

Suggestion: Serve with Mark's Italian Delight Spaghetti Sauce or use for meatball sandwiches.

Rigatoni with Meatballs

Sauce

1	28-ounce can diced tomatoes
2	tablespoons chopped garlic
1	12-ounce can tomato paste
½	teaspoon Italian seasoning
3	8-ounce cans tomato sauce
1½	tablespoons sugar
4	large cans water
4	ounces Romano cheese
¼	cup parsley flakes
	salt & pepper to taste
3	tablespoons oregano
	Parmesan cheese, optional

Mix all ingredients, excluding Romano cheese, in a large pot. Simmer for 1½ hours. Put cheese in pan the last 30 minutes of the cooking process.

Meatballs

1½	pounds ground beef, chuck or sirloin
½	teaspoon oregano
7	slices bread, toasted
½	green pepper, diced
1	egg
	salt & pepper to taste
¼	cup parsley flakes
2	tablespoons oil for frying

Crumble toast to make bread crumbs. Mix the other 6 ingredients together in a bowl. Form into 1" balls and roll in bread crumbs. Fry in oil for 10 minutes or until done. Put meatballs in sauce the last 30 minutes of the sauce's cooking time.

Prepare rigatoni noodles as directed on package. Drain noodles & plate. Pour sauce over noodles. Sprinkle with Parmesan cheese, if desired.

Servings: 8

Accompaniments: cole slaw or garden salad; garlic, Italian, or rye bread

Eggplant Parmesan with Beef

1	pound ground beef, chuck, or sirloin
½	cup onion, chopped
1/8	teaspoon garlic powder
1	28-ounce can diced tomatoes
1	8-ounce can tomato paste
½	teaspoon salt and pepper
¾	tablespoon Italian seasoning
½	teaspoon crushed cayenne red pepper
1½	tablespoons brown sugar
2	small eggplants
¾	cup cracker crumbs
1	egg
1	8-ounce package mozzarella cheese
¾	cup Parmesan cheese

Brown beef, onion, and garlic powder in a large saucepan. Drain. Add diced tomatoes, paste, salt, pepper, seasoning, red pepper flakes, and sugar to meat. Let simmer 1 hour. Peel and slice eggplant. Beat egg. Dip eggplant slices in egg and then cracker crumbs. Melt butter in skillet and brown both sides of eggplant slices. Spray a 9x13 inch casserole dish. Arrange eggplant slices in the bottom of dish. Top with sauce. Sprinkle mozzarella and Parmesan cheese over top. Bake uncovered at 350 degrees for 30 minutes.

Servings: 6

History: George B. Simpson patented the electric range in 1859.

Barbecued Pork Ribs

2 pounds country style pork ribs

   juice of 1 lemon (approximately 3 tablespoons)

2 tablespoons mustard, vinegar, and Worcestershire sauce

½ cup ketchup

¼ teaspoon red pepper flakes

1 medium onion, chopped

4 tablespoons butter

1 cup water

¼ cup brown sugar

Wash ribs and put in a large pot; cover with water. Boil for 30 minutes. Drain. Set aside. Brown chopped onion in butter for 10 minutes. Add remaining ingredients and simmer for 10 minutes. In a 9x13 dish, arrange ribs. Pour the cooked sauce over the ribs. Bake in a 350 degrees oven for 90 minutes. Serve hot.

Servings: 4

Tip: For tender, flavorful ribs begin by parboiling them in pineapple juice.

Note: Whenever barbecuing, use tongs to turn the meat. A fork should never be used. Punctures allow the juices to escape from the meat.

Corned Beef & Cabbage

4 pounds corned beef brisket

1 onion, sliced

4 potatoes, cubed

3 carrots, cut into 1" cubes

1 medium head cabbage, cut into sections

Put corned beef in a large kettle; cover with water. Place sliced onion on top of meat. Simmer in pot for 5-6 hours. If using a crock pot, cook 5-6 hours on low heat. During the last hour of cooking brisket, add carrots, potatoes, and cabbage sections. Before serving, make sure that the vegetables are tender. Serve hot.

Servings: 8

Accompaniment: cornbread

Note: This is a favorite dish served on New Year's Day. It is said that eating cabbage on this particular day will bring you good luck throughout the New Year.

Tip: When cooking cabbage, place a ½ cup of vinegar on the stove or counter to absorb the odor.

Cabbage Rolls

1	large head cabbage
2	pounds ground beef or lean pork
½	cup cooked rice
½	teaspoon salt and pepper
1	teaspoon garlic powder
1	onion, diced
1	egg

Sauce

1	15-ounce can tomato sauce
3	tablespoons flour
½	cup sugar

Put cabbage head in boiling water for approximate 3 minutes to loosen the leaves and make them pliable. Remove from water and pull off leaves. Replace cabbage leaves back in boiling water for 3 minutes; drain. Mix meat with rice, salt, pepper, garlic powder, onion, and egg. Set aside. Put about 2 tablespoons of mixture in each cabbage leaf and roll up. Secure with wooden toothpicks. Combine ingredients to make sauce. Place cabbage rolls in a 9x13 glass baking dish. Spoon sauce over rolls and cover dish with foil. Bake at 325 degrees for 1½ hours. Check every 30 minutes to see if extra liquid is needed. Add water accordingly.

Servings: 4-6

Ham Supreme

1   pound ham, ground

1   pound pork, ground

4   eggs

    dash Worcestershire sauce

2   cups graham cracker crumbs

    salt & pepper to taste

Sauce

1   10¾-ounce can tomato soup

1   cup water

1   cup brown sugar

½   cup honey

¼   cup vinegar

2   teaspoons dry mustard

Mix first 6 ingredients together and form into a loaf. Put in a 9x13 inch baking dish. Bake at 350 degrees for 1½ hours; basting frequently. Combine the sauce ingredients and put in a pan. Bring to a boil; stirring constantly. Drain meat, if necessary before applying sauce. Spoon sauce evenly over ham the last 30 minutes of baking.

Servings: 4-6

Note: A dash is equal to 1/16 teaspoon.

History: Ham is the oldest meat of civilized man.

Tex-Mex Chops

6 pork loin chops, ½" thick

2 tablespoons vegetable oil

¾ cup uncooked long grain rice

1½ cups water

1 8-ounce can tomato sauce

1 medium green pepper, chopped

2 tablespoons taco seasoning mix

½ cup shredded cheddar cheese

salt & pepper to taste

In a large skillet, brown chops in oil for 15 minutes. Sprinkle chops with salt and pepper to liking. In a greased 9x13 inch baking dish, combine rice, water, tomato sauce, and taco seasoning; mix well. Place chops over rice, top with chopped green pepper. Cover with foil and bake at 350 degrees for 1½ hours. Uncover, sprinkle with cheese and return to oven long enough to melt cheese.

Servings: 4-6

Tip: Pork chops can be kept in the refrigerator for 2-4 days; 1-3 months in the freezer.

Note: If grilled pork chops are desired, marinate chops in ½ cup soy sauce, ½ water, & ½ cup honey. Pour over chops, leave covered overnight in the refrigerator.

Pork Chop & Potato Bake

6 pork chops

2 tablespoons oil

1 teaspoon seasoned salt

1 10¾-ounce can cream of celery soup

½ cup milk

½ cup sour cream

¼ teaspoon pepper

1 32-ounce package frozen hash brown potatoes, thawed

4 ounces shredded cheddar cheese

1 6-ounce can French fried onions

Brown chops in lightly greased skillet. Sprinkle chops with ½ teaspoon seasoned salt; set aside. Combine soup, milk, sour cream, pepper, and ½ teaspoon seasoned salt. Stir in hash browns, 2 ounces of cheese, and ½ can of French fried onions. Spoon mixture into a 9x13 inch baking dish. Arrange pork chops on top of mixture. Cover with foil and bake at 350 degrees for 40 minutes. Top with remaining cheddar cheese and onions. Bake uncovered for 5 minutes longer.

Servings: 4-6

Tip: Use canola oil for frying because it has a high burning point.

Pigs in a Blanket

1   can 8 crescent rolls

8   wieners or sausage links

Wrap each roll around a wiener or sausage link. Follow baking instructions on can to brown. Provide ketchup and mustard on the side.

Servings: 6-8

Favorite school lunch item during the 1960's

History: In 1929, Oscar Mayer wieners were introduced to the general public.

Haddock with Mixed Vegetables

6   six-ounce pieces haddock

1   celery stalk, sliced

3   carrots, sliced

1   cup fresh mushrooms, sliced

2   ounces chicken broth

¼   cup white wine

2   tablespoons butter

½   lemon for juice (or 1½ tablespoons bottled lemon juice)

Sauté sliced vegetables in pan with butter and chicken broth for 20 minutes or until tender. Add the wine on the vegetables during the last 10 minutes of sautéing. Transfer vegetables to a baking dish. Place haddock on top of vegetables; squeeze the lemon juice over the fillets. Bake at 325 degrees for 20 minutes or until fish is flaky.

Servings: 6

Tip: To make homemade tartar sauce, mix sweet pickle relish & mayonnaise about ½ and ½.

Fish Fry

2 pound fillets fish (trout, catfish, whitefish, whiting, etc.)

2 cups cornmeal

½ cup vegetable oil or canola oil for frying

1 cup bottled lemon juice

½ teaspoon paprika

1 teaspoon dry mustard

1 teaspoon salt

½ teaspoon black pepper

2 large eggs, beaten

Skin and fillet fish or use fish purchased from a market or grocery store. Soak fish fillets in lemon juice for 5 minutes. Put cornmeal, dry mustard, salt, and pepper in a large plastic storage bag. Put beaten eggs in a large bowl. Season fish fillets lightly with salt and paprika; dip in egg mixture; then place individual fillets in cornmeal bag and shake. Fry fish in a large skillet with hot oil for 1 minute on each side or until golden brown.

Servings: 5-6

Accompaniments: cole slaw, hush puppies or French fries

Tip: Thawing fish fillets in milk can zap the frozen taste & make them seem even fresher.

Tip: To make homemade cornmeal, combine 1 cup cornmeal, 1 cup all-purpose flour, ½ teaspoon salt, & 4 teaspoons baking powder. Mixture can be store in a tightly covered container for 4-6 months.

Baked Salmon

1   14.75-ounce can pink salmon

1   cup bread crumbs

1   cup celery, diced

¼   cup green pepper, diced

1   small onion, minced

¼   teaspoon bottled lemon juice

1   cup evaporated milk

1   egg, beaten

Drain salmon. Debone salmon. Crumble salmon into large bowl. Mix remaining ingredients. Fold into a greased loaf pan. Bake at 350 degrees for 1 hour.

Note: The juice in canned salmon comes from the fish itself whereas tuna has oil or water added to the can.

Salmon Patties

1   14.75-ounce can pink salmon

4   eggs, slightly beaten

½   cup onion, diced

½   cup green pepper, diced

1   cup or 10 crushed saltine crackers

     salt & pepper to taste

Drain salmon and carefully debone. Combine all ingredients in a large bowl. Form into patties. Fry patties slowly in butter or hot oil about 7 minutes on each side. Patties should be golden brown. Put on paper towels or on a brown paper bag before plating.

Servings: 5-6 patties

History: Salmon & shrimp are the most popular seafood in the United States.

Venison Roast with Gravy

4 pounds venison roast

6 thick slices bacon

   salt & pepper to taste

¼ cup water

Sprinkle salt and pepper on the meat. Rub the seasonings thoroughly. Cut the bacon into square strips; lay on top of the meat. Roll up the meat; tying with butcher's string. Place in a large roasting pan. Add ¼ cup of water in the pan to keep the juices from getting too hot. Insert a meat thermometer so the tip is in the center of the roast. Bake at 325 degrees for 2½ hours. Meat thermometer should reach 175 degrees to indicate doneness. Remove roast from pan; place on a platter.

Tip: Marinate for venison: Heat 1 cup vinegar & 1 bouillon cube. Pour over venison and marinate for 2 hours to reduce the wild meat flavor.

Gravy

1½ tablespoons flour

1 cup milk

   salt & pepper to taste

Reserve 4 tablespoons of the roast's drippings. Add to a skillet. Heat until hot. Add 1½ tablespoons of flour to drippings. Let the flour brown, stirring constantly. When brown, add 1 cup milk; stirring constantly until the gravy is the right consistency. May need to add more milk if gravy is too thick. Add salt and pepper to taste. The gravy when seasoned to taste is a very flavorful addition to the venison.

Alternate cooking method: If venison is cooked in a crock pot, add pinch of apple pie spice & black pepper to cut the wild flavor.

Country Fried Venison Steak with Gravy

1½ cups all-purpose flour

¼ teaspoon black pepper

¼ teaspoon salt

8 4-ounce venison steaks

1 teaspoon garlic powder

1 teaspoon seasoned salt

¾ cup vegetable oil

medium onion, sliced

Combine 1½ cups flour and ¼ teaspoon of salt & pepper. Put in a large plastic bag. Sprinkle one side of the venison with garlic powder, and the other side with seasoned salt. Dredge the meat in the flour mixture. In a large skillet, heat ½ cup oil over medium heat. Fry steaks for 5-6 minutes per side. Add additional oil as needed while frying the steaks. When the steaks are done; it's time to make the gravy. Once the gravy is at desired thickness; return the steaks to the skillet and bring to a boil. Reduce heat, place onion slices on top of the steaks; cover and simmer for 30 minutes.

Gravy

2 tablespoons flour

pan drippings (approx. 4 tablespoons)

½ teaspoon salt & pepper

4 cups hot water

Gravy Directions

Add 2 tablespoons of flour to pan drippings in the heavy skillet. Add ½ teaspoon of salt & pepper to the mixture. Constantly stir until the flour is medium-brown and the mixture is bubbly. Slowly add the water; stirring constantly.

Pinto Beans

2 pound bag pinto beans

4-5 bacon slices

salt & pepper to taste

Pour beans on a counter top 1 cup at a time to check for small rocks or imperfections. Put checked beans in a large colander for rinsing. Rinse beans thoroughly. Put beans in a large pot; add approximately 8 cups of hot water and bacon slices. Bring mixture to a boil then reduce heat. Simmer beans for 1½-2 hours. Add salt & pepper to taste. During the cooking process, may need to add more hot water to beans. Remove cooked bacon slices if desired. Serve hot.

Servings: 10-12

Tip: Add salt after cooking beans or it will slow the cooking process.

Pinto Bean Fritters

2 16-ounce cans or equal amount of leftover beans

1 cup oil

1 small onion, chopped

4 eggs

½ green pepper, chopped

2 cups self-rising flour

1 tablespoon brown sugar

½ teaspoon salt, pepper, & garlic powder

Blend flour, eggs, pepper and salt well in a large bowl. Drain the canned beans and add to flour mixture. Add the remaining ingredients and mix well. Heat oil in a heavy skillet. Drop tablespoon-sized balls of bean mixture into the hot oil. Turn and let brown on both sides until crispy and golden. Drain and cool on paper towels. May need to repeat browning process until all the mixture is used. Keep warm on a baking sheet in the oven at 300 degrees until ready to serve.

Note: Reduce recipe ingredients according to the quantity of leftover pinto beans.

Tuna & Noodles

  1   12-ounce package noodles

  2   6-ounce cans chunk light tuna in water

  ¼   cup milk

  1   10¾-ounce can cream of mushroom soup

  1   cup bread crumbs

Cook noodles according to package directions. Drain and flake tuna. Mix drained noodles and tuna. Pour mixture into a greased glass baking dish. In a small saucepan, add milk to soup. Heat until mixed thoroughly. Pour soup mixture over tuna and noodles. Sprinkle bread crumbs on top. Bake in a 350 degrees oven for 30 minutes.

Serves: 4-6

History: Charlie the Tuna, the official mascot of Starkist tuna, made his debut in a television commercial in 1961.

Seafood Quiche

 1 pastry shell, unbaked

 ½ pound Swiss cheese, shredded

 ½ cup small shrimp

 4 ounces crab meat

 2 eggs, beaten

 1 cup whipping cream

 ½ teaspoon flour

 ¼ teaspoon salt

 ¼ teaspoon white pepper

 ¼ teaspoon cayenne pepper

 1 tablespoon sherry wine

 1 tablespoon butter, melted

Place crab meat, shrimp, and cheese in pastry shell. Mix the remaining ingredients together in a bowl. Pour mixture over seafood and cheese. Bake at 375 degrees for 40 minutes until light brown on top. Let stand 10-15 minutes before serving.

Note: Recipe can be frozen for baking at a later date.

Pork Loin with Garlic Halves

5-7   pound pork loin

4   cloves garlic, halved

1   teaspoon meat tenderizer, unseasoned

1/8   teaspoon salt

½   teaspoon black pepper

Put pork loin in baking dish. Mix together tenderizer, salt, and pepper. Rub spices on entire loin. Puncture ¼" holes in meat; insert garlic halves. Cover meat with foil. Bake in 325 degrees for 3 hours. Last 30 minutes of baking time; remove foil & increase oven temperature to 350 degrees for browning of meat. Serve hot.

Serves: 4-6

Breaded Veal Cutlets

4   6-ounce veal cutlets

1   egg

1   teaspoon water

4   tablespoons butter

1   cup bread crumbs, crumbled

1   cup flour

1   teaspoon salt & pepper

Mix salt, pepper, and flour together in a large bowl. In a separate bowl, beat egg and water together. Put crumbled bread crumbs on a plate. Dip the cutlets in the flour mixture. Cover thoroughly. Dip the floured cutlets in the egg mixture, and then in the crumbled bread crumbs. Cover completely. Allow the cutlets to dry on a rack for 20 minutes. Fry breaded cutlets in butter for 4 minutes on each side or until desired doneness.

Serves: 4

CHAPTER 5

Vegetables & Sides

Family picnic at Case's Lake in Huntington, West Virginia, 1956.

Cookin' Notes

Corn on the Cob

6 ears corn

1 tablespoon sugar

   cold water

   butter, salt, pepper to taste

Shuck the corn. Remove silk from the ears. Put corn in large pot. Cover corn with cold water. Put sugar over the corn. Cover with aluminum foil. Cook on medium high heat until water boils. Boil for 10 minutes. Drain water. Remove corn from pot and place on a platter. Serve immediately with butter, salt, and pepper.

Tip: To remove silks easily from corn, rub ears with a damp paper towel in a downward direction. Rinse each ear before placing in pot.

Note: Keep corn refrigerated in the husks; the cool temperature will keep it fresh.

Suggestion: Serve with herbed or barbecue butter.

Herbed Butter

Mix 2 teaspoons of mixed dried herbs such as basil, oregano, sage, & rosemary with 6 tablespoons softened butter.

Barbecue Butter

Mix 1 teaspoon dry barbecue seasoning with 6 tablespoons softened butter.

Grilled Parmesan Corn

     8 ears corn
    ½ cup grated Parmesan cheese
    ½ cup butter, softened
    ½ teaspoon salt
     1 tablespoon parsley, chopped

Shuck corn. Wash ears; remove silks. Combine cheese, butter, parsley, and salt in a bowl. Brush mixture on each ear. Wrap in foil; place on grill for 20-25 minutes.

Serves: 8

Fried Corn

     1 15¼-ounce can white corn
     6 slices bacon
    ¼ cup bacon grease
    ¼ teaspoon salt
    ¼ teaspoon pepper
     1 teaspoon sugar

Fry 6 slices of bacon. Set aside. Put ¼ cup bacon grease in a hot iron skillet. Empty corn with liquid into hot bacon grease. Add sugar. Cook on medium-high heat for approximately 11 minutes. Add salt and pepper to taste. Serve hot.

Servings: 4

Substitutions: 3 ears of fresh corn or 1 can of golden corn

Scalloped Corn

1   15¼-ounce can regular corn
1   15¼-ounce can cream-style corn
1   cup sour cream
4   tablespoons butter
2   eggs
1   tablespoon sugar
1   8.5-ounce box Jiffy Cornbread Mix

Mix together regular & cream corns, sour cream, butter, and eggs. Add sugar and cornbread mix. Bake in 9x13 dish at 350 degrees for 45 minutes. Serve hot.

Fried Potatoes

5-6   slices bacon
5-6   medium potatoes, cubed
      salt and pepper to taste
1   small onion, diced (optional)

Fry bacon until crispy. Remove bacon and drain on a paper towel. Fry cubed potatoes and onion in bacon grease until firm or golden brown, approximately 20 minutes. Add salt and pepper to taste (while frying potatoes). Crumble bacon on top or serve on the side.

Fried Sweet Potatoes

Save cold baked potatoes. Peel and slice ¼" thick pieces. Fry in hot fat until brown. Fried sweet potatoes can be served at any meal.

Carrot Cups

2   cups carrots, grated
½   cup soft bread crumbs
2   eggs
½   teaspoon salt
2   tablespoons butter, melted
½   cup milk
2   tablespoons parsley, finely chopped

Mix all ingredients together thoroughly. Pour into buttered custard cups. Set cups in baking pan filled with ¼"of hot water. Bake at 325 degrees for 45 minutes or until firm. Unmold and serve hot.

Serves: 4-6

History: Carrots were not the favorite vegetable of Mel Blanc, the voice of Bugs Bunny.

Hash Brown Onion Potatoes

8   cups raw potatoes, diced
4   tablespoons butter
1   8-ounce package onion soup mix
1   cup water

In medium frying pan, lightly brown potatoes in butter. Add onion soup and water. Cover with foil. Simmer for 20 minutes or until tender. Uncover and cook until liquid has evaporated. Stir occasionally. Serve immediately.

Hash Brown Potato Delight

1   32-ounce package hash browns

1   8-ounce sour cream

1   8-ounce Velveeta cheese

1   10¾-ounce can cream of chicken soup

1   small onion, diced

1   stick butter, melted

2   cups cornflakes

Put hash browns in a 9x13 baking dish. Mix sour cream, cheese, soup, onion, and ½ of the melted butter together. Pour over hash browns. Spread cornflakes on top. Dribble the other ½ of the melted butter over the cornflakes. Bake at 350 degrees for 45 minutes.

Tip: Let raw potatoes stand in cold water for 30 minutes before frying to improve crispiness.

Fried Mustard Greens

1   batch mustard greens, chopped

9   strips bacon (for approx. ½ cup fat drippings)

½   cup water

¼   teaspoon salt

Fry bacon strips until crispy. Remove bacon. Pour drippings into a measuring cup. Set aside. In a large iron skillet, add water and salt. Wash greens & chop. Place greens in skillet; cover with a lid. Cook until tender. Stir occasionally. Add ½ cup fat drippings; fry for two minutes until hot. Use bacon strips on the side or crumble over mustard greens. Serve hot.

Yields: 4

Collard Greens

 5 pounds collard greens, chopped

 8 gloves garlic, minced

 2 small onions, minced

 6 cups chicken stock or broth

 4 ham hocks

 1 tablespoon salt

½ cup sherry vinegar

10 dashes Tabasco sauce

   salt & pepper to taste

Clean and chop collard greens. In a large pot, sauté garlic & onions for 4-5 minutes. Add 1 tablespoon of salt to garlic. Add collard greens, ham hocks, chicken stock, vinegar, hot sauce, salt & pepper to taste. Cover. Cook on low heat for 3 hours. Stir occasionally. When done; remove ham hocks & discard. Serve hot.

Yields: 6

Fried Green Tomatoes

Batter:

- 1 cup cornmeal
- ½ cup flour
- 2 teaspoons baking powder
- 1 teaspoon salt
- 1 tablespoon sugar
- pinch of pepper
- 1 cup milk

Combine ingredients until thoroughly mixed. Batter should be smooth and thick.

- 5-7 green tomatoes, sliced thick
- ½ cup vegetable oil
- ½ cup bacon fat

Dip tomatoes in batter and fry in oil and bacon grease. Drain on paper towels. Serve hot.

Servings: 4-6

Suggestion: Batter could be used to make onion rings.

Note: Sunlight doesn't ripen tomatoes, warmth does. Keep tomatoes with stems pointed down & they will stay fresh longer.

Creamed Potatoes

6 medium potatoes

1 cup boiling water

1 12-ounce can cream or 1 cup milk

2 tablespoons butter

   salt and pepper to taste

¼ teaspoon chopped parsley

Pare and cut potatoes in slices. Add water and cook 5 minutes in a covered pan on high heat. Add cream and seasoning. Cover again and cook slowly until sauce thickens. Sprinkle with parsley. Serve immediately.

Tip: To keep potatoes from budding, put an apple in the potato bag.

Baked Rice & Mushrooms

1 cup rice, uncooked

1 14-ounce can beef broth

1 10¾-ounce can cream of mushroom soup

1 tablespoon butter

1 7-ounce can sliced mushrooms

Combine all ingredients. Mix thoroughly. Place in an 8" baking dish. Cover with foil. Bake at 350 degrees for 1 hour. Serve hot.

Granny's Sweet Potatoes

  6 sweet potatoes

  ½ stick butter

  3 tablespoons brown sugar

  3 tablespoons maple syrup

Peel potatoes. Slice in round shapes. Cook in water approximately 20 minutes or until done. In a skillet, put melted butter, sweet potato rounds, syrup, and brown sugar. Fry until potatoes are brown. Serve warm.

Sweet Potatoes with Marshmallows

  1 cup milk

  1 teaspoon vanilla

  3 tablespoons sugar

  4 tablespoons butter

  2 29-ounce cans sweet potatoes

  1/8 teaspoon cinnamon

  1/8 teaspoon nutmeg

  1 tablespoon orange juice

  20 miniature marshmallows

Drain sweet potatoes and mash. Set aside. Scald milk. Add vanilla, sugar, and butter. To mashed sweet potatoes, add nutmeg, cinnamon, and juice. Mix thoroughly. Stir in scalded milk. Beat until fluffy. Pour ½ of the potato mixture into a lightly greased 9x13 casserole dish. Add 10 miniature marshmallows. Top with remaining potato mixture. Bake at 350 degrees for 25 minutes or until very hot. Add 10 miniature marshmallows on top and brown.

Serves: 8

Tip: Marshmallows won't dry out, if frozen.

Bourbon Sweet Potatoes

- 5 medium sweet potatoes
- 1 teaspoon vanilla
- ¼ cup butter
- 1 teaspoon cinnamon
- 2 eggs
- 1½ ounces bourbon

Bake sweet potatoes wrapped in foil for 1 hour or until tender. Peel & beat with a mixer for 5 minutes. Add butter, eggs, vanilla, cinnamon, and bourbon. Continue mixing until smooth. Pour into a greased baking dish.

Topping for sweet potatoes

- ¼ cup butter, melted
- ¾ cup light brown sugar
- 3 tablespoons flour
- ½ cup pecans, chopped

Mix ingredients together well. Sprinkle over potatoes. Bake at 350 degrees for 30 minutes. Serve hot.

Tip: Sweet potatoes will not turn dark if put in salted water immediately after peeling.

Potato Cakes

2 cups mashed potatoes

3 teaspoons baking powder

1 egg, beaten

½ teaspoon salt

2 tablespoons butter

oil for frying

1 cup all-purpose flour

1 teaspoon caraway seeds (optional)

Combine potatoes, egg, butter, and caraway seeds. Beat until fluffy. Sift the flour, baking powder, and salt together; add to potato mixture. Knead lightly until thoroughly mixed. Roll on a lightly floured board to ¼" thickness. Cut in squares and cook in a greased frying pan over low heat until golden brown (approximately 5 minutes on each side). Serve immediately.

Suggestion: Serve with plenty of butter or sour cream.

Cheesy Zucchini with Bread Crumbs

2 pounds zucchini

4 tablespoons butter

¼ cup vegetable oil

1¼ cups white rice, cooked

¼ cup grated Parmesan cheese

2 eggs, beaten

2 tablespoons melted butter

¼ cup grated sharp cheddar cheese

1 cup bread crumbs

salt & pepper to taste

Fix rice according to package directions. Set aside. Steam zucchini until tender; chop into small pieces. In a pot, combine oil and butter. On low heat, melt butter. Add cooked rice and chopped zucchini. Sauté until golden brown; stirring frequently. Stir in cheese until melted. Add seasonings & remove from heat. Stir in eggs quickly; pour into greased baking dish. Spread bread crumbs on top. Drizzle butter on bread crumbs. Broil until light brown and bubbly. Serve hot.

Servings: 6-8

Zucchini Fritters

2	cups shredded zucchini
2	eggs
¼	cup onion, finely chopped
½	teaspoon salt
2	tablespoons grated Parmesan cheese
1 1/3	cups all-purpose flour
2	teaspoons baking powder
	oil for deep frying

In a large bowl, combine zucchini, eggs, onion, salt, and grated cheese. Gradually stir in flour and baking powder until combined thoroughly. Drop by heaping tablespoons into deep hot oil. Fry for 1½-2 minutes. Drain on paper towels. Serve warm. Sprinkle with additional Parmesan cheese, if desired.

Servings: 12 medium fritters

Squash Fritters

3   cups squash, grated

2   tablespoons minced onion

1   egg
    oil for frying

2   tablespoons sugar
    salt and pepper to taste

6   tablespoons flour

Salt squash; let drain in colander. Squeeze the moisture from the squash. Combine all ingredients except the oil in large bowl. Mix well. Fry a small amount at a time in skillet. Make sure to brown both sides. Serve hot.

Note: Zucchini is a member of the cucumber & melon family.

Deviled Eggs

 10 eggs

   salt and pepper to taste

 ½ teaspoon mustard

 1/3 cup sweet pickle relish

  2 tablespoons mayonnaise

  2 tablespoons Thousand Island Salad Dressing

   chives, parsley flakes, olive slice, or paprika (egg toppings)

Place 10 eggs in pan. Cover eggs with cold water and add 4 tablespoons of salt to the water. Boil on medium-high heat for 15 minutes. Turn off heat and drain water. Run cold water over eggs and add more salt to the water. Roll and crush each egg on counter top or cutting board. Rinse eggs before cutting into halves. Remove yolks and put in a bowl. In the same bowl, add salt and pepper to taste, mustard, relish, mayonnaise, and salad dressing. Mix thoroughly. Put in an icing bag and use a #32 tip or use a zipped plastic bag and cut tip. Fill each egg. Sprinkle one of the egg toppings to decorate each egg half. Refrigerate 2 hours before serving.

Yields: 20 eggs

Tip: The salt added to the water while cooking and afterwards will help in the removing of the egg shells.

Tuna Stuffed Eggs

10 eggs

 4 tablespoons salt

 1 6-ounce can tuna, drained

 3 tablespoons sweet pickle relish

 1 cup mayonnaise

 1 tablespoon mustard

    salt & pepper to taste

Place 10 eggs in pan. Cover eggs with cold water and add 4 tablespoons of salt to the water. Boil on medium high heat for 15 minutes. Turn off heat and drain water. Run cold water over eggs and add more salt to the water. Roll and crush each egg on counter top or cutting board. Rinse eggs before cutting into halves. Remove yolks and put in a bowl. Drain tuna and flake. Stir in 3 tablespoons sweet pickle relish, 1 cup mayonnaise, and 1 tablespoon mustard. Add to mashed egg yolks. Mix thoroughly until smooth. Add more mayonnaise if dry. Season with salt and pepper. Fill egg whites with egg mixture. Chill before serving.

Note: Best to use canned tuna in water not oil for this recipe.

Cole Slaw

2	cups shredded cabbage
½	cup chopped parsley flakes
½	cup finely sliced green onions
2-3	tablespoons sugar
3	tablespoons vinegar
2	tablespoons vegetable oil
1	teaspoon salt

Combine vegetables. Blend remaining ingredients, stirring to dissolve sugar. Pour over vegetables; toss. Refrigerate for 2 hours before serving.

Servings: 6

Suggestion: Garnish top with green pepper rings or paprika.

History: In 1912, Richard Hellman began marketing his bottled mayonnaise.

Seven Day Slaw

1	medium head cabbage
1	medium red onion
1/3	cup sugar
1	cup vegetable oil
1	cup vinegar
2	tablespoons sugar
½	teaspoon dry mustard
¼	tablespoon salt
¼	tablespoon black pepper

Shred cabbage and slice onion thinly. Toss with 1/3 cup of sugar. Mix remaining ingredients in a pot and bring to a boil. Pour boiling mixture over cabbage and onion. Let mixture set for 5 minutes. Mix thoroughly. Chill in refrigerator for 2 hours before serving.

Note: This recipe is called "Seven Day Slaw" because without any mayonnaise, it will last easily for seven days.

History: In 1912, coleslaw became classified as a side dish.

Glazed Beets

3	15-ounce cans whole beets
5	teaspoons sugar
1	tablespoon all-purpose flour
¼	teaspoon salt
1	tablespoon vinegar

Drain beets, reserving 2/3 cup juice. In a large skillet, combine the sugar, flour, and salt. Stir in vinegar and the reserved beet juice until smooth. Bring to a boil. Cook and stir for 2 minutes or until thickened. Add beets; reduce heat. Cook uncovered for 5 minutes or until thoroughly heated.

Servings: 6

Whipped Beets

2 cups hot beets, cubed

½ cup French dressing

½ cup green onions, minced

1 cup sour cream, whipped

Mix hot beets with dressing. Place in bowl. Top with whipped sour cream. Sprinkle with minced green onions.

Note: Beets are a great source of folate (folic acid).

Baked Beans

2 16-ounce cans pork & beans

5 strips bacon

1 medium onion, diced

3 tablespoons light brown sugar

1 tablespoon mustard

½ cup ketchup

Combine pork & beans, onion, sugar, mustard, and ketchup in a large bowl. Mix thoroughly. Pour into a 1½ quart casserole dish. Top with bacon strips. Cover with foil. Bake at 350 degrees for 45-50 minutes.

Baked Beans with Hamburger

1   pound hamburger

1   medium onion, diced

½   cup ketchup

1   pound or 16-ounce can pork & beans

2   tablespoons light brown sugar

1   teaspoon chili powder.

   oil for frying

Fry hamburger and onions in 2 tablespoons of oil until brown. Mix pork & beans and the remaining ingredients together. Bake in 350 degrees oven for 15-20 minutes.

Ginny's Potato Salad

6   medium potatoes, cooked & diced

4   hard boiled eggs, chopped

1   small green pepper, diced

1   small onion, finely chopped

1/3   cup sweet pickle relish or chopped sweet pickles

1/3   cup mayonnaise

1/3   cup sour cream

2   teaspoons chopped canned pimento (4-ounce jar)

1   tablespoon sugar

1   teaspoon salt

1   teaspoon black pepper

½   teaspoon celery seed

Combine potatoes and remaining ingredients in large bowl. Mix thoroughly. Chill for several hours before serving.

Suggestion: Garnish with carrot curls or parsley flakes, if desired.

Tip: If a light bulb breaks in a socket, put a half uncooked potato onto the jagged glass, unscrew the bulb & toss.

Scalloped Potatoes

8-10 medium potatoes, sliced

1 medium onion, diced

1 10¾-ounce can cheddar cheese soup

¾ soup can of milk

1 tablespoon butter

2 tablespoons dried chives

1 tablespoon parsley flakes

1 teaspoon salt

1 teaspoon black pepper

Peel and slice potatoes in a round glass baking dish. Sprinkle potatoes with salt and pepper. Dice onion and put in baking dish with potatoes. Mix ingredients thoroughly. Set aside. In a saucepan, put soup, milk, and butter. Cook on medium heat until hot; stirring frequently. Pour over potatoes and onions. Spread chives and parsley over top of mixture. Bake at 350 degrees for 1 hour. Check doneness by inserting a fork easily through potatoes. Remove from oven; cover with foil until ready to serve.

Serves: 6-8

Scalloped Spinach

2 tablespoons chopped onion

¼ cup grated American cheese

2 eggs, beaten

½ cup buttered bread crumbs

½ cup milk

2 cups cooked spinach or 2 16-ounce packages chopped frozen spinach

Cook spinach; drain. Put in a 1 quart greased casserole dish. Add onion, eggs, milk, & cheese to spinach. Spread bread crumbs evenly over spinach mixture. Bake at 350 degrees for 20 minutes. Serve hot.

Green Beans with Slivered Almonds

2   14.5-ounce cans green beans, French style

1   10¾-ounce can cream of mushroom soup

1   4-ounce can pimentos

½   cup slivered almonds (2.25-ounce package)

1   6-ounce box of French onion rings

Heat green beans in a saucepan until hot. Drain and put in a round casserole dish. Add soup and pimentos. Sprinkle with almonds; top with onion rings. Bake at 300 degrees for 35 minutes. Serve hot.

Cauliflower and Peas

1   medium head cauliflower

3   stalks celery, thinly sliced

1   15-ounce can sweet peas

Dressing Ingredients

¾   cup sour cream

¾   cup mayonnaise

1   small onion, diced

1   teaspoon salt

1   teaspoon black pepper

Drain peas. Put in a large bowl. Wash cauliflower and break into pieces. Wash celery stalks; slice thinly. Add cauliflower and celery to bowl. Set aside. Mix dressing ingredients together in a separate bowl. Pour over vegetables. Mix thoroughly. Chill 2 hours before serving.

Tip: To keep cauliflower white while cooking, add a little milk to the water.

Sautéed Snow Peas & Mushrooms

1 tablespoon butter

¾ pound fresh mushrooms, sliced

1 8-ounce can water chestnuts, drained & sliced

¾ pound fresh snow peas

In a heavy skillet, melt butter over medium heat. Sauté mushrooms & water chestnuts until tender. Add snow peas & sauté until peas turn bright green. Do not overcook. Serve immediately.

Serves: 6

History: The 1st frozen TV dinner contained turkey, peas & sweet potatoes.

Ham Fried Rice

½ yellow onion, chopped

½ pound diced cooked ham

2½ cups cooked rice

2 tablespoons soy sauce

¼ teaspoon salt

1 teaspoon sugar

2 scrambled eggs

2 green onions, chopped

Brown onion and ham in skillet. Add cooked rice, soy sauce, salt, and sugar. Add scrambled eggs to skillet. Mix well. Garnish with chopped green onions

Serves: 4

Tip: To add extra flavor & nutrition to rice, cook it in liquid reserved from cooking vegetables.

Three-Vegetable Medley

8 ounces fresh cauliflower, separate into pieces

8 ounces fresh squash, sliced

8 ounces fresh broccoli, cut into pieces

   butter (to sauté vegetables)

¼ cup Parmesan cheese

1 2.25-ounce package toasted almonds (½ cup)

   juice from lemon half (1½ tablespoons)

   salt and pepper to taste

Wash all vegetables. Sauté vegetables separately in butter until al dente. Remove pan from heat and gently combine vegetables together. Add cheese and almonds to vegetables. Return to high heat and sauté quickly for 3-4 minutes. Try not to overcook vegetable mixture. Add lemon juice and season with salt and pepper.

Serves: 6-8

Note: Al dente ("to the tooth" in Italian) means tender crisp, not overcooked; vegetables should remain firm in texture.

Mushroom Roll-Ups

1 pound fresh mushrooms, chopped

1 medium onion, chopped

2 tablespoons butter or margarine

½ cup sour cream

1 tablespoon all-purpose flour

½ teaspoon salt

¼ teaspoon black pepper

1 egg

1 tablespoon water

½ cup dry bread crumbs

½ teaspoon seasoned salt

2 tablespoons melted butter

8 egg roll wrappers

Sauté mushrooms and onions in butter until onions are transparent, about 15 minutes. Combine sour cream, flour, salt, and pepper. Add to mushroom-onion mixture. Continue to cook, stirring constantly, until mixture bubbles, about 2 minutes. Beat egg with water and set aside. Mix bread crumbs with seasoned salt. Place egg roll wrapper on cutting board. Place about ¼ cup filling 1" from end. Roll up. Brush egg mixture to seal seam. Roll in seasoned bread crumbs and place seam side down on ungreased baking sheet. Repeat with remaining wrappers. Drizzle melted butter over the 8 egg rolls. Bake in 350 degrees oven for 12-15 minutes, until golden brown. Serve hot with a dollop of sour cream topped with chopped chives or parsley.

Servings: 8

Tip: When stems & caps are attached snugly, mushrooms are truly fresh.

Turnip Greens

3 pounds turnip greens

1 teaspoon salt

4 cups water

1 ham hock

In a large pot, simmer ham hock in water for 50 minutes. Wash greens. Add salt & greens to pot. Cook until tender. Drain. Serve hot.

Serves: 4-6

Tip: Cook diced potatoes with your turnips; it will reduce the strong flavor.

Baked Asparagus

1 10¾-ounce can cream of mushroom soup

1 10¾-ounce can cream of celery soup

2 8-ounce cans water chestnuts, drained & sliced

1 6-ounce can French fried onions

1 batch asparagus

Wash asparagus. Line the bottom of a 9x13 baking dish with asparagus. Top with sliced water chestnuts. Mix together soups. Pour evenly over asparagus & chestnuts. Bake at 350 degrees for 30 minutes. Remove from oven; sprinkle the onions on top. Return to oven & bake for 10 minutes or until crisp. Serve hot.

Tip: Do not wash asparagus before storing in the refrigerator.

Italian Eggplant

- 1 medium eggplant, pared and cut into ½" slices
- ½ cup butter, melted
- ¾ cup dry crushed bread crumbs
- ¼ teaspoon salt
- 1 13-ounce jar spaghetti sauce (or use recipe in cookbook)
- 1 7-ounce can sliced mushrooms
- 1 tablespoon oregano
- 1 cup mozzarella cheese, shredded

Mix salt & bread crumbs together. Place in a bowl. Dip eggplant slices in butter then bread crumbs. Place in a baking dish. Spread spaghetti sauce evenly over top. Sprinkle with oregano leaves and cheese. Bake at 350 degrees for 30 minutes. Serve hot.

Fried Eggplant

- 1 large eggplant, pared and cut into ½" slices
- 2 eggs
- 1 cup bread crumbs, crushed
- 1/8 teaspoon nutmeg

Place crushed bread crumbs in a large plastic bag. Set aside. Mix eggs and nutmeg in a bowl. Dip eggplant in egg mixture. Place individual slices in bread crumbs bag to cover. Put in deep fryer until golden brown. Serve hot with favorite dipping sauce.

History: Thomas Jefferson is credited with introducing eggplant to North America.

Fried Cabbage

4   cups chopped cabbage

6   slices bacon, diced

1   medium onion, chopped

    salt, pepper, and garlic powder

Fry bacon until crisp. Add cabbage and onion. Season to taste with salt, pepper, and garlic powder. Cook at medium heat about 15 minutes. Stir frequently.

Cooked Cabbage with Bacon

1   medium head cabbage

6   slices bacon

    water

    salt & pepper to taste

Cut ends off cabbage head. Cut cabbage in half; remove the stalk. Wash halves thoroughly. Cut cabbage into desired pieces. Put cut cabbage into a large pot. Cover with water. Add salt & pepper to taste. Place bacon slices in pot. Cook cabbage and bacon on medium heat for 1½ hours or until tender. Serve hot.

Suggestion: Serve with hot cornbread.

CHAPTER 6

Breads

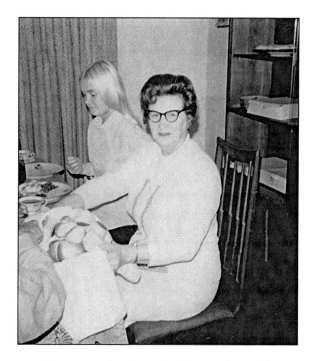

Great-grandmother, Lucille, posing with
her homemade rolls.
Thanksgiving, 1970

139

Cookin' Notes

Refrigerator Rolls

  2   cups boiling water

 ½   cup sugar

  1   tablespoon salt

  2   tablespoons vegetable shortening

  2   ¼-ounce packages dry yeast

 ¼   cup warm water

  2   eggs, beaten

7-8   cups flour

Stir together boiling water, sugar, salt, and shortening. Cool until lukewarm. Dissolve yeast in ¼ cup warm water. Add to sugar mixture. Add beaten eggs. Stir in 4 cups of flour and beat with wooden spoon until smooth. Stir in 3-4 cups more flour until dough in fairly stiff. Place in greased bowl. Turn dough to grease thoroughly. Cover with wax paper or plastic wrap; place in refrigerator. Dough will keep for 6-7 days. To bake, shape rolls according to preference. Place in greased muffin pan. Let rise, covered, until doubled in bulk (about 1-1½ hours.) Bake 15-20 minutes at 425 degrees.

Yields: 2 dozen cloverleaf rolls or 4 dozen plain rolls

Sour Cream Rolls

1 ¼-ounce package dry yeast
½ cup warm water
1 8-ounce carton sour cream
½ cup sugar
2 sticks butter or margarine, melted
2 eggs beaten
4 cups flour
1 teaspoon salt

In a large bowl, dissolve yeast in warm water. Blend sour cream and sugar with ½ cup melted butter (1 stick). Stir into yeast mixture with eggs, flour, and salt. Knead lightly on floured surface. Place in greased bowl; turn until all the mixture is coated. Let rise covered, until double in bulk. Divide into 4 portions, and roll each into a 12 inch circle. Brush each circle with 2 tablespoons of butter. Cut into 12 wedges and roll up from wide end, shaping into crescents. Place on greased baking sheet and let rise until double in bulk. Bake at 375 degrees for 10-12 minutes or until browned.

Yields: 4 dozen rolls

Tip: Rolls may be frozen after shaping in crescents. Remove from freezer to baking sheets (3 hours before serving time) to thaw and rise. Bake as indicated.

Tag's Butter Rolls

1	cup boiling water
½	cup shortening
¼	cup warm water
1	¼-ounce package dry yeast
4½	cups sifted flour
½	cup sugar
1	egg

In a small bowl, pour boiling water over shortening; stir until shortening is melted. Cool to lukewarm. In small bowl, sprinkle yeast over warm water stirring until dissolved. In large bowl, sift together flour and sugar; stir in cooled shortening, yeast, and egg. Beat vigorously with wooden spoon until well-blended. Knead in bowl until dough is smooth. Cover and let rise in warm place for 1 hour. Punch down roll mixture and let stand for several hours. To bake, shape rolls according to preference. Place in greased muffin pans. Bake at 425 degrees for 15-20 minutes or until browned.

Tip: To keep bread crust from getting hard, set a pan of water in the oven while the bread is baking.

Angel Biscuits

5   cups all-purpose flour

3   tablespoons sugar

3   teaspoons baking soda

1   teaspoon salt

¾   cup Crisco vegetable shortening

1   ¼-ounce package dry yeast

½   cup warm water

2   cups buttermilk

Dissolve yeast in warm water (let stand according to directions). Combine dry ingredients in a bowl. Set aside. Combine buttermilk and yeast mixture together, and add to dry ingredients. Stir until moistened. Cover and chill in refrigerator. Dough will keep in refrigerator for several days. Roll out dough and cut with biscuit cutter (a little flour may be needed to make dough easier to work with). Place on slightly greased baking sheet. Use fingers to put melted margarine over biscuits. Let rise for about ½ hour or longer. Bake at 400 degrees for 12 minutes or until brown. Remove from oven. May need to separate the biscuits by hand.

Yields: approx. 4 dozen (depending on thickness of dough)

Tip: Roll biscuit dough thin then fold before cutting. Makes biscuits flaky in the center & will split open easily for buttering.

History: Crisco vegetable shortening was introduced by Procter & Gamble in 1911.

Alabama Biscuits

- 2 cups sifted flour
- 1 teaspoon salt
- 3 teaspoons baking powder
- 1 ¼-ounce package yeast
- ¼ cup warm water
- 1 teaspoon sugar
- 3 tablespoons shortening, melted
- ¾ cup milk

Mix yeast and warm water and stir until dissolved. Sift all dry ingredients together. Melt shortening and add to warm milk. Add shortening/milk mixture to yeast and water. Mix well. Combine with dry ingredients and stir until well-blended.

To bake: On lightly floured surface, roll biscuit dough ½ inch thick. Cut with biscuit cutter. Brush tops with melted butter and place one on top of another. Let rise until double in bulk. Bake 15-20 minutes in 450 degrees oven.

Tip: Baking powder, unopened, will keep 6 months; opened will keep 3 months.

Bulk Biscuits

  1   ¼-ounce package dry yeast
  ¼   cup warm water
 3½   cups Martha White All-Purpose Flour
  1   cup water
  2   tablespoons vegetable oil
 1½   teaspoons salt

Grease two large baking sheets; set aside. Dissolve yeast in water in large bowl. Add remaining ingredients; blend well. Cover and let rise in warm place for 45 minutes or until double in bulk. Stir down. Drop by tablespoons onto prepared baking sheets. Cover and let rise in warm place for 40 minutes or until double in bulk. Preheat oven to 425 degrees. Bake 18-20 minutes or until golden brown.

Yields: 24 biscuits

Tip: Flour unopened will keep up to 12 months; opened will keep 6-8 months.

Cathead Biscuits

 10   slices bacon
  2   ounces Crisco vegetable shortening
  6   cups self-rising flour
  6   cups milk
  1   level teaspoon salt

Fry bacon in skillet until crisp. Crumble bacon & set aside. In a large bowl, mix flour, milk, and salt. Use a measuring cup (one cup) to scoop batter onto nonstick cookie sheet. Keep spacing between scoops of batter. Bake at 325 degrees for 30-35 minutes. Check on biscuits about 20 minutes into the baking process. Remove from oven & crumble crisp bacon on top. Serve hot.

Serves: 6-8

Suggestion: Serve with butter, jelly, or creamy gravy.

Mexican Cornbread

1	11-ounce can corn & peppers (drained)
1½-2	cups corn meal
½	cup oil
1	cup milk
2	eggs
3	tablespoons dried onion
2	cups shredded cheddar cheese
3	hot peppers, chopped

Mix together all ingredients and pour into 13x9 baking pan. Preheat oven to 350 degrees. Bake for 40-45 minutes.

Tip: If you forget to preheat the oven, simply turn on the broiler for 5 minutes.

Delicious Cornbread

1	cup cornmeal
1	cup all-purpose flour
¼	cup vegetable oil
1	tablespoon sugar
½	teaspoon baking soda
1	teaspoon baking powder
1	teaspoon salt
1	cup buttermilk
2	eggs, beaten

Mix ingredients and pour into greased baking pan. Preheat oven to 400 degrees. Bake for 20 minutes or until brown.

Tip: To make buttermilk, add 1 tablespoon of vinegar or lemon juice to 1 cup of sweet milk.

French Bread

1¾   cups warm water

2   ¼-ounce packages dry yeast

1   tablespoon vegetable oil

2   teaspoons salt

4½ to 5½ cups flour

1   egg white, beaten

1   tablespoon water

Mix all ingredients (except egg white or tablespoon of water) for 8 minutes. Let rise for 45 minutes. Punch down and roll out two 10x15 sections. Roll sections up like jelly rolls. Let rise for 1½ hours. Slash top and baste with egg white and 1 tablespoon of water mixture. Bake at 400 degrees for 25 minutes

Tip: Add an egg wash to make French bread really brown. French bread must have a high temperature to bake properly.

Basic Bread

1 quart milk

1 cup solid Crisco vegetable shortening

1 cup sugar

2 ¼-ounce packages dry yeast

6 cups all-purpose flour

1 tablespoon salt

1 heaping teaspoon baking powder

1 teaspoon baking soda

additional all-purpose flour

butter, melted

Combine milk, lard, and sugar in sauce pan; scald and cool to lukewarm. Dissolve yeast in ½ cup of lukewarm milk mixture. Add dissolved yeast and 6 cups of flour to milk mixture; stir until dough is in consistency of cake batter. Cover and let rise in a warm place until doubled in bulk. Add salt, baking powder, baking soda, and enough flour to make dough stiff. (At this stage, dough may be stored four-five days in the refrigerator and used as needed). Divide dough into quarters; shape into loaves and place in 4 greased 8x4 inch loaf pans. Cover and let rise in warm place until doubled in bulk. Bake at 350 degrees about 35 minutes or until loaf is brown on top. Brush top lightly with melted butter.

Tip: When working with dough, don't flour your hands. Coat them with oil to prevent them from sticking to the dough.

Delicious Orange Bread

1   cup sugar

½   cup butter

2   eggs

1   cup sour cream

    orange rind, grated (called orange zest)

2   cups sifted cake flour

1   teaspoon baking soda

½   cup sugar

    juice of 1 orange

Mix sugar and butter until creamy. Add eggs, sour cream, and the orange rind. Sift flour and baking soda. Mix into other ingredients. Bake at 350 degrees for 50 minutes in two medium bread pans. Mix together sugar and orange juice; pour over bread while still hot in pans. Cool for 10 minutes and invert on serving plate.

Note: 1 orange = ½ cup juice

Raisin Casserole Bread

   1 cup milk
   ½ cup sugar
   1 teaspoon salt
   ¼ cup margarine (1/2 stick)
   ½ cup warm water
   2 ¼-ounce packages dry yeast
   1 egg
  4½ cups unsifted flour
   1 cup seedless raisins

In saucepan, scald milk; stir in sugar, salt, and margarine. Cool to lukewarm. Measure warm water into large bowl, sprinkle or crumble in yeast; stir until dissolved. Stir in lukewarm milk mixture, egg and 3 cups of flour to make a stiff batter. Cover and let rise in a warm place, free of draft, until double in bulk (approx. 1 hour.) Stir batter down. Beat in raisins. Turn into 2 greased 1 quart casserole dishes. Bake at 350 degrees for 40-45 minutes.

Yields: 2 loaves

Tip: To see if old yeast is still good, put a teaspoon in a cup of warm water & add 1 teaspoon of sugar. If it foams & rises in 10 minutes, it is still good for baking.

Apricot Nut Bread

1½ cups dried apricots (approx. ½ pound)
1   cup water
2½ cups all-purpose flour
5   teaspoons baking powder
½   teaspoon baking soda
½   teaspoon salt
½   cup sugar
½   cup chopped nuts (walnuts or pecans)
1   egg
1   cup buttermilk
2   tablespoons shortening, melted

Wash apricots and place in saucepan with 1 cup of water. Boil until apricots are soft, about 10 minutes. Drain, if there is any liquid left. Cool and chop apricots. Sift flour once before measuring. Sift flour, baking powder, baking soda, salt, and sugar together. Add nuts to flour mixture. Beat egg well, add milk and stir into flour mixture. Add melted shortening; mix thoroughly. Fold in chopped apricots. Pour into well-greased bread loaf pans (8x4x3). Let stand for 20 minutes. Bake at 350 degrees for 65 -70 minutes.

Banana Nut Bread

¾   cup butter

1½ cups sugar

3   eggs, separated

5   large bananas, mashed (approx. 1½ cups)

3   cups all-purpose flour

1½ teaspoons baking soda

½   cup sour cream

½   cup milk

¾   cup pecans, finely chopped

¾   teaspoon salt

Grease two bread loaf pans and set aside. Mix butter and sugar together until creamy. Add egg yolks, one at a time, beating well after each addition. Add bananas, mixing well. Measure ½ cup milk and add sour cream to fill the cup. Sift together the flour, soda, and salt. Add the flour and milk mixture alternately to banana mixture, ending with the flour. Add nuts and mix well. Beat egg whites until they stand in stiff peak; fold carefully into banana batter. Divide batter evenly between two greased bread loaf pans, filling each to within ¾ "of the top. Bake at 325 degrees for 1 hour.

Tip: Bread made with fruit & nuts should be tested with a straw in the center. Tester should come out perfectly clean when bread is done.

Pineapple Zucchini Bread

3 eggs
1 cup vegetable oil
2 cups sugar
2 teaspoons baking soda
2 teaspoons vanilla extract
¼ teaspoon baking powder
2 cups shredded zucchini
1 cup raisins, optional
1 8-ounce can crushed pineapple (drained)
3 cups all-purpose flour
1½ teaspoons cinnamon
1 teaspoon salt
¾ teaspoon nutmeg
1 cup chopped pecans

Beat eggs, oil, sugar, and vanilla until thick. Stir in zucchini and pineapple. Mix in all other dry ingredients. Pour into 5x9 pans. Bake at 350 degrees for 1 hour.

Zucchini Bread

3   eggs, well-beaten

3   teaspoons vanilla

1   cup vegetable oil

2¼ cups sugar (1¼ cups brown sugar & 1 cup white sugar)

2   cups zucchini, peeled & grated

3   cups sifted all-purpose flour

¼   teaspoon baking powder

1   teaspoon salt

1   teaspoon baking soda

3   teaspoons cinnamon

2   tablespoons orange rind, grated (orange zest)

1   cup chopped nuts

Combine all wet ingredients in large bowl; mix thoroughly. Sift together all dry ingredients into same bowl as wet ingredients; mix thoroughly. Pour into 2 greased and floured loaf pans. Bake at 325 degrees for 1 hour.

Note: Bread wrapped in aluminum foil and stored in a zipped plastic bag will last in the freezer for 3 months.

Six-Weeks Bran Muffins

1   15-ounce box Raisin Bran cereal

3   cups sugar

5   cups all-purpose flour

5   teaspoons baking soda

2   teaspoons salt

4   eggs, beaten

1   quart buttermilk

1   cup vegetable oil

   Optional - extra cup raisins, golden or regular

Combine Raisin Bran cereal, extra raisins, sugar, flour, soda, and salt in a very large bowl; mix well. Add eggs, buttermilk, and oil; mix well. Put in a covered container and refrigerate overnight. This batter is ready to use. Do not stir anymore. Lightly grease and flour muffin pans and fill ¾ full. Bake at 400 degrees for 15-20 minutes.

Yields: 48-54 muffins

Note: This batter will stay good in the refrigerator for 6 weeks, hence the name.

CHAPTER 7

Desserts

My sister, Amber, celebrating her 3rd birthday.

Erica celebrating her 5th birthday with family & friends.

Cookin' Notes

Old Fashioned Pie Crust

1 cup Crisco vegetable shortening

3 cups sifted plain flour

1 teaspoon salt

5 tablespoons water

1 tablespoon white vinegar

1 egg

In large bowl, work Crisco and salt into flour with fingers. Combine in a small bowl, the tap water, vinegar, and 1 egg. Beat until smooth. Make a well in the flour mixture and pour egg mixture in all at once. Mix well. This pastry will not get tough by continued handling. Divide dough into 3 parts. Roll out between two 12 inch sheets of wax paper. When rolled out to the correct size, peel back paper and flour each side of dough. Put dough into pie pan. Bake at 350 degrees for 20 minutes.

Tip: Leftover pie dough can be used to create a good snack or treat for children.

Helen's Never-Fail Pie Crust

4 cups plain flour

1¾ cups Crisco vegetable shortening

2 teaspoons salt

1 tablespoon sugar

1 egg

½ cup water

1 tablespoon vinegar

In small bowl, beat together egg, water, and vinegar. In large bowl, mix flour, Crisco, salt, and sugar. Pour egg mixture into flour mixture and blend thoroughly. Chill for 15 minutes or longer. Divide mixture by 5, roll dough out, and flour both sides. Place in pie pans. Bake at 350 degrees for 20 minutes.

History: The frozen pie crust was introduced in 1962.

Custard Pie

½ cup sugar

1 cup milk

1 tablespoon flour

2 eggs

   nutmeg (sprinkle on top)

Beat eggs. Add sugar, flour, and milk; stir well. Pour in pie crust and sprinkle with nutmeg. Bake at 250 degrees slowly until done. Use toothpick method to tell when finished.

Delightfully Banana Dessert

1   12-ounce box vanilla wafers

1   20-ounce can crushed pineapples

¼   cup butter, melted

1   8-ounce container Cool Whip

1¾   cups powdered sugar

1   6-ounce jar cherries, chopped

1   teaspoon vanilla extract

1   2.25-ounce package crushed pecans

2   eggs

4   large bananas, sliced

½   cup butter, softened

Crush wafers. Add ¼ cup butter & mix. Pour into a 9x13 glass dish. In a mixing bowl, beat eggs, sugar, vanilla, & ½ cup softened butter at high speed for 10 minutes. Pour over crushed wafers. Slice bananas in a bowl & sprinkle with lemon juice. Mix well-drained crushed pineapples with bananas. Spread evenly in baking dish. Top with Cool Whip. Sprinkle generously with crushed pecans & chopped cherries. Refrigerate for 3 hours before serving.

Baskin Robbins Pie

1   8-ounce package Philadelphia Cream Cheese

1   cup sugar

1   8-ounce container Cool Whip

1   3.9-ounce package instant chocolate pudding

1   14-ounce box graham cracker pie crust

1   cup shaved chocolate

Using large baking dish, follow instructions on box to make graham cracker pie crust. Bake 10 minutes and let cool. Follow instructions to make chocolate pudding; let cool. In bowl, mix cream cheese, sugar, and ½ Cool Whip. Layer in baking dish on top of crust.

> cream cheese mixture
>
> chocolate pudding
>
> remaining Cool Whip

Sprinkle top with shaved chocolate. Chill in refrigerator for 1 hour.

Tip: To save mess when making a graham cracker crust, place in plastic bag & roll with a rolling pin.

Basic Pecan Pie

3   eggs, slightly beaten

1   cup sugar

1   cup light or dark corn syrup

1   tablespoon corn oil margarine, melted

1   teaspoon vanilla

1   cup pecan halves

1   unbaked (9 inch) pie shell

In medium bowl, stir eggs, sugar, corn syrup, margarine and vanilla until well-blended. Stir in pecans. Pour into pie shell. Bake at 350 degrees for 50-55 minutes or until knife inserted halfway between center and edges comes out clean. Cool on rack.

Yields: 8 servings

Alternatives:

Chocolate Pecan Pie

Reduce sugar to 1/3 cup. Melt 4 squares (1-ounce each) semi-sweet chocolate with margarine.

Sour Cream Pecan Pie

Stir ¼ cup sour cream into eggs until blended.

Tip: Can substitute crushed corn flakes for pecans. Both rise to the top and provide a crunchy surface.

Coconut Cream Pie

   1 cup sugar

1/3 cup all-purpose flour

  ¼ teaspoon salt

  1 5-ounce can evaporated milk

2¼ cups milk

  3 eggs, separated

  2 tablespoons butter

  1 teaspoon vanilla

  1 cup (3½-ounces) flaked coconut

  1 baked 9" pie crust

  ½ teaspoon cream of tartar

  3 tablespoons sugar

  ¾ teaspoon corn starch

Combine sugar, flour, and salt. Gradually add milk and evaporated milk stirring until blended. Cook over medium heat stirring constantly, until mixture thickens and comes to a boil. In separate bowl, beat egg yolks until thick. Gradually stir in ¼ of hot mixture into yolks. Blend and then add to remaining hot mixture. Cook over medium heat, stirring continuously for 1 minute. Remove from heat and stir in butter, vanilla, and coconut. Pour into cooked pie crust. In separate bowl, beat egg whites (at room temperature) and cream of tartar at high speed until foamy. Combine 3 tablespoons sugar and cornstarch; add a tablespoon at a time to egg whites, beating until stiff peaks form and sugar dissolves (2-4 minutes). Spread topping over pie filling. Bake at 450 degrees for 5 minutes.

Tip: To prevent crust from becoming soggy, sprinkle crust with powdered sugar.

Lemon-Meringue Pie

1	baked 9″ pie shell
1¼	cups sugar
6	tablespoons cornstarch
2	cups water
1/3	cup lemon juice
3	eggs, separated
3	tablespoons butter
1½	teaspoons lemon extract
2	teaspoons vinegar

Mix sugar, cornstarch together in top of double boiler. Add the 2 cups of water. Combine egg yolks with lemon juice, beat, and add to hot mixture. Cook until thick over boiling water for 25 minutes. Starchy taste will be eliminated. Add lemon extract, butter, and vinegar; stir thoroughly. Pour into deep, 9″ pie shell. Let cool. Cover with meringue and brown in oven.

Note: Use the Never-Fail Meringue recipe on the next page.

Tip: Meringue will not shrink if you spread it on the pie so it touches the crust on each side & bake in a moderate oven.

Never-Fail Meringue

1   tablespoon cornstarch

2   tablespoons cold water

½   cup boiling water

3   egg whites

6   tablespoons sugar

1   teaspoon vanilla

    pinch of salt

Blend cornstarch and cold water in a saucepan. Add boiling water and cook, stirring until clear and thickened. Let stand until completely cold. With electric beater at high speed, beat egg whites until foamy. Gradually add sugar, vanilla, and pinch of salt. Beat until stiff peaks are forming and sugar dissolves (approx. 10 minutes).

Tip: Egg whites for meringue should be set out for room temperature before beating; they can be beaten to a greater volume.

Blueberry Pie

2   graham cracker pie crusts

1   12-ounce Cool Whip

1   14-ounce can condensed milk

4   tablespoons bottled lemon juice

1   quart blueberries

Gently fold first 4 ingredients together, and then fold in blueberries. Divide into 2 pie shells. Chill for 2 hours or overnight. May freeze.

Tip: Blueberries are rich in Vitamins C & E.

Red Cherry Pie

¾–1   cup sugar

4   tablespoons flour

¼   teaspoon almond extract

½   teaspoon cinnamon

2½   cups sour red cherries and juice (14.5-ounce can)

2   tablespoons butter

1   unbaked 9" pie crust with top

Combine first 4 ingredients in saucepan. Stir in cherries and juice. Cook on medium heat, stirring constantly, until mixture thickens and boils. Pour into uncooked 9" pie crust. Dot with butter. Cover with top; make slits. Bake at 425 degrees for 30-40 minutes or until browned and juice bubbles through slits in crust.

Tip: Cut drinking straws into short lengths & insert through slits in pie crust to prevent juice from running over in the oven. It allows the steam to escape.

Tip: Brush cream then sprinkle sugar on top of pie crust; browns beautifully.

Apple Pie

¼ cup sugar

1 tablespoon flour

½ teaspoon cinnamon

   dash of salt

1 12.5-ounce can apple pie filling

¼ cup butter

¼ cup brown sugar

½ cup sifted flour

1 unbaked 9" pie crust with top

Combine in a large bowl the first 4 ingredients. Toss lightly with apples. Spoon into 9" pie crust. Combine butter, brown sugar, and ½ cup flour. Sprinkle over pie filling. Cover with lattice or regular top. Bake at 425 degrees for 35-40 minutes or until brown.

Tip: If the juice from the apple pie runs over in the oven, shake some salt on the spill. It will cause the juice to burn to a crisp so it can be removed easily.

Million Dollar Pie

1 8-ounce container Cool Whip

1 14-ounce can condensed milk

1 20-ounce can crushed pineapple (undrained)

½ cup bottled lemon juice

½ cup chopped pecans

2 baked 9" pie shells

Mix together all ingredients. Pour into 2 baked 9" pie shells. Cool in refrigerator.

Striped Delight

- 1½ cups graham cracker crumbs
- 2 tablespoons milk
- ¼ cup granulated sugar
- 1 8-ounce container Cool Whip
- 1/3 cup butter, melted
- 3½ cups cold milk
- 2 3.9-ounce packages chocolate pudding
- ¼ cup granulated sugar
- 1 8-ounce package cream cheese, softened

In a saucepan, combine graham cracker crumbs, ¼ cup sugar, and butter. Stir frequently until blended thoroughly. Press mixture in the bottom of a greased 9x13" baking pan. In a bowl, beat cream cheese with ¼ cup sugar & milk. Fold in ½ of the Cool Whip. Spread over crust. Using 3½ cups cold milk, prepare pudding. Pour pudding mixture over cream cheese layer. Chill 2 hours or overnight in the refrigerator. Before serving, spread remaining Cool Whip over pudding.

Yields: 10 servings

History: Cool Whip was invented in 1965.

Strawberry Cream Cheese Pie

1   8-ounce package cream cheese

½   cup sugar

½   container Cool Whip (8-ounce tub)

1   baked 9" pie shell or graham cracker crust, cooled

1   3-ounce package Jello strawberry gelatin

1   cup boiling water

1   pint strawberries, halved and sweetened with sugar

Whip cream cheese until soft; beat in sugar. Blend Cool Whip into cream cheese mixture. Line bottom and sides of pie pan with mixture; mounding high at edges. Dissolve gelatin in boiling water. Drain syrup from strawberries into bowl; add cold water. Add ½ of strawberry/water mixture to gelatin. Chill until thickened; fold in strawberries. Spoon into cream cheese lined pie pan without covering the narrow rim of cheese filling around edge. Chill until gelatin is set (approx. 3 hours).

History: Jello was invented in 1897 by Pearl Bixby Wait of Leroy, New York.

Strawberry Pinwheel Pie

1　9" graham cracker pie crust

1　cup sour cream

1　cup milk

1　3.9-ounce package vanilla instant pudding

2　cups fresh strawberries, sliced

½　cup water

½　cup sugar

1½　tablespoons cornstarch

Mix sour cream, milk, and vanilla instant pudding. Beat until thoroughly mixed and thickened. Pour into 9" graham cracker pie crust.

Glaze Recipe

Combine ½ cup fresh strawberries, ¼ cup water in small saucepan and simmer for 3 minutes. In small bowl, combine sugar, cornstarch, and ¼ cup water. Mix well and combine with berries in saucepan. Cook for 1 minute stirring constantly.

Put 1½ cups of fresh strawberries over top of vanilla filling. Shape strawberries like a pinwheel. Cover with the glaze. Chill for 3 hours.

History: The idea of Strawberry Socials caught on by the late 1800's Northern communities had adopted the custom almost as their own and expanded the ways in which strawberries could be used. Often strawberries were blended with custard pies and local ladies vied for the honor of "Best Strawberry Pie Maker in Town." This recipe is a new take on an old favorite.

Red Velvet Cake

2½   cups all-purpose flour

1   cup buttermilk

1½   cups vegetable oil

1   teaspoon baking soda

1   teaspoon vanilla extract

¼   cup red food coloring (21-ounce bottle)

1½   cups granulated sugar

1   teaspoon unsweetened cocoa powder

1   teaspoon white vinegar

2   large eggs

1   teaspoon salt

1/3   pound butter softened (1 1/3 sticks)

1   8-ounce package cream cheese, softened

1   16-ounce (1 pound) box confectioner's sugar

2   cups chopped pecans

Heat oven 350 degrees. Mix together sugar and oil at medium speed. Add milk, vinegar, and vanilla. Sift flour, soda, cocoa, and salt; add to mixture. Add eggs 1 at a time. Add food coloring and blend. Spray three 9" round cake pans with nonstick coating. Pour batter equally into 3 pans and bake for 20 minutes. Test for doneness with a toothpick. Cool layers in pans on wire rack for 10 minutes. Carefully remove layers from pans to racks to cool completely.

Frosting Directions

Combine butter, cream cheese, and confectioner's sugar in a bowl. Beat until fluffy, fold in 1½ cups of pecans. Use to fill and frost cake when it's cool. Decorate top of cake with remaining ½ cup of pecans. Refrigerate at least 1 hour before serving.

Yields: 10-15 servings

Best Chocolate Cake

¼ cup cocoa

2 cups sugar

2 cups all-purpose flour

1 stick butter

1 cup water

½ cup vegetable oil

2 eggs

½ cup buttermilk

1½ teaspoons baking soda

1 teaspoon vanilla extract

Preheat oven to 350 degrees. Combine first 3 ingredients in a large bowl; mix thoroughly. Melt butter with water and oil in small sauce pan over medium heat; bring to boil. Pour over dry ingredients; mix well. Add eggs, ½ cup buttermilk, baking soda, vanilla and blend thoroughly. Pour into greased 18x11 rectangle cake pan. Bake for 25 minutes.

Frosting

1 16-ounce box powdered sugar

¼ cup cocoa

1 stick butter

1/3 cup buttermilk

1 teaspoon vanilla extract

1 cup chopped nuts (optional)

Melt butter in saucepan. Mix in buttermilk and vanilla. In a large bowl, mix sugar, cocoa, and nuts. Pour butter mixture over dry ingredients; blend thoroughly. Apply frosting to warm cake.

Tip: Use icing as soon as it is made; all icings will form a crust or become very stiff quickly.

Cocoa Cake

    4 tablespoons cocoa

   ½ cup cooking oil

    1 stick butter

    1 cup water

Combine & bring to a boil. Add the following ingredients:

    2 cups granulated sugar

    2 cups all-purpose flour

    2 eggs, well beaten

    1 teaspoon baking soda

   ½ teaspoon salt

    1 teaspoon vanilla extract

    1 cup buttermilk

Continue to heat; stirring frequently. Remove from stove & pour into a greased & floured 9x13" dish. Bake at 375 degrees for 30 minutes.

Icing

    4 tablespoons cocoa

    6 tablespoons milk

    1 stick butter

    1 teaspoon vanilla extract

    1 16-ounce box confectioner's sugar

Combine cocoa, milk & butter. Bring to a boil. Stir in sugar & vanilla. Spread icing on cooled cake.

Watergate Cake

- 1   cup club soda
- 1   3.9-ounce box pistachio instant pudding
- ½   cup chopped pecans (2.25-ounce package)
- 1   18.25-ounce box white cake mix
- 1   cup vegetable oil
- 3   eggs

Mix all ingredients for cake mixture except pecans. Mix 4 minutes. Fold in nuts. Pour into greased baking pan. Bake at 350 degrees for 45 minutes. Cool cake before applying frosting.

Frosting

- 1   3.9-ounce box pistachio instant pudding
- 1   cup coconut flakes
- ¼   cup cold milk
- 1   8-ounce tub Cool Whip
- 1   cup pecans, chopped finely

Mix pudding with cold milk, and follow directions on box. Fold in coconut and cool whip. Apply icing to cooled cake. Sprinkle top of cake with finely chopped nuts.

Tip: To achieve better baking results, preheat pans.

Lemon Delight Cake

1 18.25-ounce package lemon cake mix

½ cup oil

1 cup orange juice

1 3.9-ounce package instant lemon pudding

4 eggs

In a large bowl, combine cake mix, oil, orange juice, and instant pudding. Add eggs 1 at a time. Beat until smooth. Grease and flour 10" tube pan. Pour mixture into pan. Bake at 350 degrees for 60-70 minutes or until cake springs back when touched with finger. If desired, frost with your favorite lemon icing.

Tip: To keep icing moist & to prevent cracking; add a pinch of baking soda to icing.

Apple Sauce Cake

1½ cups apple sauce

½ cup Crisco vegetable shortening

2 cups sugar

1 egg

2½ cups all-purpose flour

½ teaspoon salt

½ cup boiling water

½ teaspoon cinnamon

½ teaspoon cloves

½ teaspoon allspice

1 cup raisins

1 cup chopped nuts (almonds or pecans)

2 teaspoons baking soda

Cream shortening and add sugar gradually. Add beaten egg and apple sauce. Sift flour before measuring, and use a little of the same flour to sift over the fruits and nuts. Sift the remaining flour with salt and spices. Dissolve baking soda in boiling water. Add flour mixture alternately with the water into the shortening mixture. Add floured raisins and nuts; mix well. Pour into greased baking pan. Bake at 350 degrees for 1 hour.

Tip: A pinch of salt added to applesauce will give it a richer flavor.

Easy and Delicious Cheese Cake

1   8-ounce package cream cheese

1   8-ounce container Cool Whip

1/3   cup of sugar

½   teaspoon vanilla

1   12.5-ounce can pie filling (cherry or your choice)

1   14-ounce graham cracker pie crust (can be store-bought)

Let cream cheese soften and Cool Whip get to room temperature. Bake graham cracker pie crust for 5 minutes at 350 degrees. Let cool. In a large bowl, mix cream cheese, Cool Whip, sugar and vanilla. Mix ingredients until creamy and fluffy. Pour into pie crust. Top with pie filling. Refrigerate until firm.

Note: This is my favorite cheese cake recipe. It is really delicious. The recipe was given to me by a great family friend, Maxine Hannon.

Cream Cheese Carrot Cake

- 2 cups sugar
- 1½ cups vegetable oil
- 4 eggs
- 2 cups all-purpose flour
- 3 cups carrots, grated
- 1 cup chopped nuts (almonds, walnuts, or pecans)
- 2 teaspoons baking powder
- 2 teaspoons baking soda
- 1 teaspoon salt
- 2 teaspoons cinnamon

In a large, bowl mix oil and sugar. Add eggs one at a time and beat. Sift together flour, baking powder, baking soda, salt, and cinnamon. Add flour mixture to oil mixture. Add carrots. Pour into greased baking pan. Bake at 350 degrees for 1 hour. Let cake cool.

Frosting

- 1 8-ounce package cream cheese
- 1 stick butter (room temperature)
- 1 16-ounce box confectioner's sugar
- 1 teaspoon bottled lemon juice

Frosting Directions

In a large bowl mix, cream cheese, butter, confectioner's sugar, and lemon juice. Beat on high until frosting is creamy. Apply to cooled carrot cake.

Virginia's Sour Cream Pound Cake

2 sticks butter, softened

3 cups sugar

¼ teaspoon baking soda

6 eggs

3 cups all-purpose flour

1 cup sour cream

1 teaspoon vanilla

Sift flour and soda together. Cream margarine and sugar together. Add eggs. Stir in sour cream and flour; mix thoroughly. Pour into greased tube pan. Bake at 325 degrees for 1½ hours.

Tip: To cut a fresh cake, use a sharp, thin knife dipped in water.

Peg's Sour Cream Pound Cake

½ pint sour cream

2 eggs

1 cup sugar

1 stick butter

2 cups all-purpose flour

1 teaspoon baking soda

1 teaspoon baking powder

1 teaspoon vanilla extract

Filling

1 12-ounce package chocolate chips

¼ cup brown sugar

1 cup pecans, chopped (2 small packages)

Cream together sour cream, eggs, sugar, butter, and vanilla. Sift flour, baking soda, and baking powder; add to cream mixture. Beat slowly. Divide mixture in half. In separate bowl, add ingredients for filling; divide in half. In a greased tube pan, layer ½ of cake batter then ½ of filling mix. Repeat procedure with batter & filling. Bake at 350 degrees for 50-60 minutes.

Tip: To soften brown sugar, heat in the oven for several minutes.

Eva's County Fair-Winning Pound Cake

1	cup butter
½	cup Crisco vegetable shortening
3	cups sugar
3½	cups flour
5	eggs
1	cup milk
½	tablespoon baking powder
½	tablespoon salt
½	tablespoon vanilla extract
½	tablespoon lemon extract

Mix shortening, butter, and sugar in large bowl. Add eggs 1 at a time. Add vanilla and lemon to milk. Add baking powder & salt to flour. Combine flour & milk mixture. Pour into greased tube or loaf pan. Bake at 250 degrees for 1½ hours or until cake springs back when touched with finger.

Chess Cake

- 1　18.25-ounce box Duncan Hines Yellow Cake Mix
- 1　stick butter, melted
- 1　egg, beaten
- 1　16-ounce box confectioner's sugar (save some to sprinkle on top of cake)
- 1　8-ounce cream cheese
- 3　eggs, beaten
- 1　teaspoon vanilla

Mix in large bowl, yellow cake mix batter, melted butter, & 1 beaten egg. Mix with fork; press into greased and floured 9x13 baking pan. In separate bowl, mix confectioner's sugar, cream cheese, 2 beaten eggs, and vanilla. Beat for 5 minutes. Pour sugar mixture over cake mixture in baking pan. Bake at 350 degrees for 35 minutes. Sprinkle top with confectioner's sugar.

Tip: Use a sandwich bag as a perfect mitt for greasing your pans.

Sour Cream Coffee Cake

- 1 stick butter
- 1 cup sugar
- 2 eggs
- ½ pint sour cream
- 1½ teaspoons vanilla
- 2 cups all-purpose flour
- ¼ teaspoon salt
- ¼ teaspoon baking soda

Filling

- ¼ cup of sugar
- 1 teaspoon cinnamon
- ½ cup chopped nuts (almonds, walnuts, or pecans)

In a large bowl, mix butter & the remaining ingredients. Beat thoroughly. Separate batter in half. In large bowl, mix all ingredients for filling and blend. In a greased & floured tube pan, layer ½ cake batter then ½ filling mixture. Repeat the procedure. Bake at 350 degrees for 50-60 minutes.

Blueberry Pudding Cake

1½   cups blueberries

½   cup brown sugar

1   tablespoon butter

¼   cup Crisco vegetable shortening

½   cup sugar

1   egg

1¼   cups all-purpose flour

¼   teaspoon salt

1½   teaspoons baking powder

1/3   cup orange juice

Combine blueberries, brown sugar, and butter in a saucepan. Simmer for 5 minutes. Spread in greased 8" square cake pan. Cream shortening and sugar. Add egg and beat well. Sift together dry ingredients and add alternately with orange juice. Spoon batter evenly over berries. Bake at 350 degrees for approx. 60 minutes. Serve warm.

Blueberry Banana Snack Cakes

1¼   cups sugar

2/3   cup butter, melted

¼   cup buttermilk

2   eggs

1   teaspoon vanilla

3   medium-ripe bananas, mashed (2 cups)

2   cups all-purpose flour

¾   teaspoon baking soda

1/8   teaspoon salt

1   cup fresh or frozen blueberries

powdered sugar, if desired

Preheat oven 350 degrees. In a large bowl, combine sugar, butter, buttermilk, eggs, and vanilla. Beat at medium speed until creamy (2-3 minutes.) Add bananas and continue beating until mixed. Beat at low speed until moistened. By hand, stir in blueberries. Spoon into paper lined muffin cups. Bake for 25-30 minutes or until toothpick is inserted and center comes out clean. Cool before serving. Sprinkle tops with powdered sugar.

Blackberry Cake

1½ cups butter (or 1 cup butter, ½ cup margarine)
2 cups sugar
6 large eggs
1½ cups mashed fresh blackberries or 15-ounce can, drained
6 tablespoons buttermilk
2 teaspoons baking soda
1 teaspoon baking powder
1 teaspoon cinnamon
1 teaspoon cloves
1 teaspoon nutmeg
1 teaspoon allspice
2 teaspoons vanilla
3 cups all-purpose flour

Cream butter and sugar. Add eggs one at a time, beating well after each addition. Add blackberries, milk, vanilla, and dry ingredients. Mix well. Pour into 3 greased and floured 8 inch layer cake pans. Bake at 350 degrees until top springs back when touched by finger (20-30 minutes). Fill layers with cream cheese filling. Frost with favorite caramel icing.

Filling

1 8-ounce package cream cheese
1 stick butter
1 teaspoon vanilla
1 16-ounce box confectioner's sugar

Combine all ingredients for filling recipe and mix thoroughly. If too thick to spread, add a little milk.

History- This recipe is over 60 years old, but it is still a favorite today!

Note: Blackberries help reduce inflammation and protect against chronic disease.

Almost Heaven West Virginia Cake

1   18.25-ounce box yellow cake mix

2   3.9-ounce boxes vanilla pudding

2   10-ounce packages frozen strawberries

1   8-ounce carton Cool Whip

2   cups toasted almonds

Cook pudding according to direction on box; cool. Cook cake mix according to directions on box; bake in 2 round cake pans. Cool and spilt crosswise to make four round layers. In a deep bowl, alternate cake, strawberries, pudding, whipped topping, and almonds. Cover and refrigerate for 6 hours.

Serves: 8

History: West Virginia became the 35th state in the Union on June 20, 1863.

You Won't Have a Bite Left

2   cups plain flour

2   sticks butter, melted

1   cup chopped pecans

1   8-ounce cream cheese (softened)

1   8-ounce container Cool Whip (save extra for topping)

1   cup confectioner's sugar

3   3.9-ounce boxes chocolate instant pudding

4½ cups milk

Mix flour, melted butter, and chopped pecans. Put in 13x9x2 inch pan. Bake at 375 degrees for 15-20 minutes or until browned. Let cool. In large bowl, beat cream cheese, Cool Whip, and confectioner's sugar. Spread on crust. Mix together chocolate pudding and milk. Blend until thick. Spread on second layer; top with Cool Whip.

Tip: Dusting nuts with flour before adding to batter will keep them from settling on the bottom of the pan.

Punch Bowl Cake

1   18.25-ounce package yellow cake mix

1   8-ounce container Cool Whip (may need extra for topping)

1   3.9-ounce instant vanilla pudding

1   quart strawberries

3   bananas

1   13.5-ounce can chunk pineapples (drained)

1   15-ounce can peaches (drained)

    coconut, flaked

Bake cake as directed on box; cool. Prepare pudding as directed on box; cool. In a large bowl, crumble cake and place as bottom layer in bowl. Follow with a layer of pudding, one of fruit, and one of Cool Whip. Continue layering for about 3 layers, alternating fruit. End with a layer of Cool Whip. Sprinkle top with coconut. Cover and refrigerate for 5 hours.

History: In 1947, Pillsbury & Betty Crocker introduced cake mixes.

Old-Fashioned Strawberry Shortcake

2   1-pint baskets strawberries, washed and hulled
½   cup plus 2 teaspoons granulated sugar
1   cup heavy cream
2   cups unsifted all-purpose flour
1/3 cup sugar
4   teaspoons baking powder
½   teaspoon salt
1/8 teaspoon nutmeg
½   cup butter, softened
1   egg
1/3 cup milk

Slice all but 1 strawberry into a bowl; sprinkle with the ½ cup of sugar and let stand at room temperature. If desired, crush berries, slightly. Whip cream with 2 teaspoons of sugar; refrigerate. Mix flour, 1/3 cup sugar, baking powder, salt and nutmeg in large bowl. Cut in butter until mixture resembles course meal. Beat together egg and milk, add to flour mixture and stir just until blended. Pat into a 9 inch round on a greased baking sheet. Bake in 450 degrees oven 15 minutes, or until golden brown. Let cool about 2 minutes, then spilt shortcake with serrated knife into 2 layers. Spread a little softened butter on the bottom of cut side and the top of top layer. Place bottom layer on a serving plate. Spread with 2/3 of whipped cream and top with 2/3 of strawberries and syrup. Add top layer of shortcake, spread with almost all of remaining whipped cream. Top with remaining strawberries and syrup. Garnish with a dollop of whipped cream and reserved whole strawberry.

Yields: 6-8 servings

Truly Different Cup Cakes

    4   squares unsweetened chocolate
    2   sticks margarine or butter
    ¼   tablespoon butter flavoring
   1½   cups pecans, chopped (3 small packages)
   1¾   cups sugar
    1   cup self-rising flour
    4   large eggs
    1   tablespoon vanilla

Melt chocolate and butter in a saucepan. Add butter flavoring and pecans; stir to coat pecans. Remove from heat. Combine sugar, flour, eggs, and vanilla. Mix gently. Do not beat. Add chocolate/nut mixture; mix gently without beating. Put into 18 baking cups set in muffin pans. Bake at 325 degrees for 30-35 minutes.

Note: 1 square baking chocolate = 1 ounce
History: 1957 margarine sales take the lead over butter.

Pumpkin Cream Cheese Roll

3 eggs

1 cup sugar

2/3 cup canned pumpkin

1 teaspoon baking soda

1 teaspoon cinnamon

½ teaspoon nutmeg

¾ cup all-purpose flour

Filling

1 8-ounce package cream cheese

4 tablespoons butter, softened

1 cup powdered sugar

1 teaspoon vanilla

Additional supplies needed

wax paper, aluminum foil, clean linen towel (not terry cloth), powdered sugar, and sieve.

In a large bowl, beat eggs and sugar. Beat in remaining cake ingredients. Grease a 10x15 jelly roll pan. Line pan with waxed paper, then grease and lightly flour the waxed paper. Pour batter into the pan and spread evenly. Bake at 350 degrees for 15 minutes. ** Cake cooks fast so watch it carefully to avoid burning the edges. While cake is baking, sprinkle powdered sugar heavily over kitchen towel, using a sieve or sifter. Turn hot cake onto the towel. Remove waxed paper. Trim off burnt or crusty edges. Sprinkle more powdered sugar over the hot cake; quickly roll up with towel inside. Let cake cool completely, about 30 minutes. While cake is cooling, prepare filling by beating together all ingredients until smooth and creamy. Unroll cooled cake; spread with the filling mixture. Roll up cake with filling on the inside. Wrap in waxed paper and then foil. Refrigerate or freeze. Before serving, slice cake and sprinkle with powdered sugar.

Potato Chip Cookies

1   pound butter

1   cup sugar

2   teaspoons vanilla

3½ cups self-rising flour

1   cup crushed potato chips

Cream margarine and sugar. Add other ingredients and mix. Drop by tablespoons on ungreased cookie sheet. Bake at 350 degrees until edges are browned about 10-12 minutes.

Yields: 8 dozen cookies

Sugar Cookies

3¾ cups sifted all-purpose flour

1½ teaspoons baking powder

1   teaspoon salt

1   cup butter

1½ cups sugar

2   teaspoons vanilla

2   eggs

Sift flour with baking powder, salt, and set aside. Cream butter, sugar, and vanilla until light and fluffy. Add eggs one at a time, beat well after each egg. Slowly mix in dry ingredients. Drop mixture by tablespoons on cookie sheet. Brush with milk and sugar on top of cookies. Bake at 375 degrees for 8-9 minutes.

Tip: When rolling cookie dough, sprinkle board with powdered sugar instead of flour. Too much flour makes dough heavy.

No Oven Chocolate Oatmeal Cookies

2   cups granulated sugar

1   teaspoon vanilla extract

½   cup milk

½   cup peanut butter, smooth

¼   cup cocoa

3   cups oats

1   stick butter

Bring sugar, milk, cocoa, & butter to a boil (approx. 1 minute). Remove from stove. Add vanilla, peanut butter, and oats. Stir & let cool. After cooling, mix ingredients again & drop by tablespoon on wax paper. Let stand until firm.

Easy Cobbler Recipe

1   cup self-rising flour

1   cup sugar

¾   cup milk

8   ounces butter, melted

1   21-ounce can pie filling (cherry, apple, peach, or strawberry)

Pour butter into square baking pan. Mix all other ingredients together (except pie filling) & beat well. Pour into buttered pan. Pour pie filling over mixture. Bake at 350 degrees until browned.

History: Frozen pie crust was introduced in 1962.

Peach Cobbler

1½ tablespoons butter, melted

2   cups all-purpose flour

¼   teaspoon baking powder

2   cups granulated sugar

3   eggs

    pinch of salt

1   29-ounce can sliced peaches, drained

Put melted butter in a medium-sized baking dish. Combine remaining ingredients (except peaches) and pour batter in dish. Place peaches on top of the batter. The batter will rise up & around the peaches. Bake at 350 degrees for 30 minutes. Reduce oven temperature to 300 degrees & continue to bake for 30 minutes or until golden brown. Serve hot.

Suggestion: Top pieces of cobbler with vanilla ice cream.

Cherries Jubilee

2 cups graham cracker crumbs (14-ounce box)

½ cup butter

6 tablespoons confectioner's sugar

½ teaspoon unflavored gelatin (1/4-ounce package)

In a large bowl, mix ingredients. Pour into lightly buttered 8x14 pan. Put in refrigerator to cool while making the filling.

Filling

2 envelopes Dream Whip

1 cup sugar

1 cup cold milk

1 8-ounce package cream cheese (room temperature)

4 ounces cream cheese (room temperature), cut regular package in half

½ teaspoon vanilla

pinch of salt

2 12.5-ounce cans cherry pie filling

Mix all ingredients for filling except the cherries. Spread the filling over prepared crust. Add cherries on top. Chill for 2 hours.

Peanut Butter Fudge

1   16-ounce package light brown sugar

1   5-ounce can evaporated milk

4   tablespoons butter (½ stick)

1   teaspoon cider vinegar

1   teaspoon vanilla extract

1   18-ounce jar chunky peanut butter (1½ cups)

Butter 8x8 baking pan; set aside. In a large saucepan, mix first 4 ingredients over medium heat. Bring to boil, stirring constantly. Set candy thermometer in place and continue to cook without stirring until temperature reaches 238 degrees or soft ball stage (when small amount of mixture dropped into very cold water forms a soft ball which flattens on removal from water.) Remove from heat. With wooden spoon, beat until mixture begins to thicken and cools. Stir in vanilla extract and peanut butter until well-blended. Pour into prepared pan. Refrigerate fudge until firm. When firm, cut into six strips; then cut each strip crosswise into six squares. Store in tightly covered container.

Easy Peanut Butter Fudge

3   cups sugar

1   cup milk

6   tablespoons peanut butter

3   tablespoons white syrup

1   cup nuts, chopped

In large saucepan, boil sugar, milk, and syrup until mixture forms softball when dropped into very cold water. Remove from heat. Pour into medium-size bowl; let stand until cool. Beat until creamy. Add nuts and pour into buttered 8x8 baking pan. Chill until firm.

Delicious Chocolate Fudge

4   cups granulated sugar

1   14-ounce can evaporated milk

1   stick butter

1   16-ounce package chocolate morsels

6   marshmallows

1   cup English walnuts, chopped

1   teaspoon vanilla

Mix milk & sugar together. Cook in a saucepan for 8-9 minutes after it begins to boil. Stir frequently. Stir in butter and cook for approximately 45 seconds. Remove from heat. Add chocolate, vanilla, marshmallows, & chopped nuts. Mix by hand until set. Pour into buttered pans. Cut into squares when fudge is firm.

Quick & Easy Chocolate & Peanut Butter Fudge

1   12-ounce bag semi-sweet chocolate chips

1   12-ounce jar peanut butter, smooth or chunky

1   14-ounce can sweetened condensed milk

In a large bowl, melt chocolate chips & peanut butter in microwave on high for 4 minutes. Remove & stir thoroughly. Add milk; stirring until blended. Pour mixture into an 8x8" pan lined with waxed paper. Refrigerate until fudge is chilled & ready to cut into 1" pieces.

Note: May top fudge with choice of nuts before chilling.

Black Walnut Fudge

1½ cups granulated sugar

1   cup brown sugar

1/3 cup light cream

1/3 milk

2   tablespoons butter

1   teaspoon vanilla

½   cup black walnuts, chopped

Butter sides of heavy 2 quart sauce pan. In pan, combine sugars, cream, milk, and butter. Heat over medium heat, stirring constantly until sugars dissolve and mixture comes to a boil. Cook to soft ball stage (238 degrees). Stir only if necessary. Immediately remove from heat; cool to lukewarm without stirring. Add vanilla. Beat vigorously until fudge becomes very thick and starts to lose its gloss. Quickly stir in black walnuts; spread in buttered shallow pan. Cut in squares when firm.

Tip: One pound of granulated sugar equals 2 cups.

Appalachian Rock Candy

2   cups sugar

2   cups white Karo syrup

1   cup water

    candy flavoring (favorite flavor such as mint, cinnamon, etc.)

    food coloring (choose red, green, orange)

    confectioner's sugar for coating

Cook first 3 ingredients to hard crack stage. Add coloring and flavor. Pour in pan to form and cool. Break when cooled; coat with confectioner's sugar.

Divinity Candy

3   cups granulated sugar

2   egg whites, beaten until stiff

1   cup cold water

1   teaspoon vanilla extract

2   tablespoons white vinegar

1   cup black walnuts, chopped

1/8   teaspoon salt

Combine sugar, vinegar, water & salt in sauce pan. Heat slowly, stirring until sugar is dissolved then cook rapidly until it reaches 234 degrees on candy thermometer or hard ball forms in cold water. Beat eggs until stiff, but not dry. Add sugar mixture very gradually to beaten eggs; beating vigorously to prevent eggs from cooking into a ball. Beat until mixture is creamy & holds it shape. Add vanilla & nuts. Beat well; pour onto unbuttered wax paper in a 9x13" baking dish. Cool then cut into squares. Candy will pull off wax paper when cooled.

Note: Can decorate top with candied fruit, if desired.

Symphony Bars

1   19.8-ounce box brownie mix

3   Symphony candy bars (4.2-ounce bars)

1   2.25-package chopped walnuts (1/2 cup)

Follow brownie directions on box. In a 9x13 baking pan, layer brownie mixture with crushed candy bars. Bake in 325 degrees oven for 30 minutes. Top with chopped walnuts.

Yields: 10 servings

For Testing Purposes: Duncan Hines Family Style Brownie Mix was used.
Note: These brownies are simple to make & absolutely delicious!

Date Bars

- 1 cup sugar
- 3 eggs, beaten
- 1 cup all-purpose flour
- ¼ teaspoon salt
- 1 teaspoon baking powder
- 1½ cups dates, sliced
- 1 teaspoon baking soda
- 1 cup pecans
- 1 teaspoon vanilla
- confectioner's sugar for topping

Mix all ingredients together and pour into baking dish. Bake at 350 degrees for 30 minutes. When cooled, top with confectioner's sugar.

*Tip: If substituting honey for sugar, use **half** the amount in the recipe.*

Fruit Medley

- 1 21-ounce can peach pie filling
- 2 15-ounce cans fruit cocktail, drained
- 1 20-ounce can pineapple chunks, drained
- 1 15-ounce can mandarin oranges, drained
- 2 firm bananas, sliced

Mix all ingredients together. Chill & serve.

Banana Split Bars

2 extra ripe bananas, peeled

2 cups all-purpose flour

1 cup sugar

¾ teaspoon baking soda

½ teaspoon salt

½ teaspoon cinnamon

1 13.5-ounce can crushed pineapples (undrained)

2 eggs

½ cup vegetable oil

1 teaspoon vanilla extract

¼ cup maraschino cherries, drained and halved

Puree bananas (1 cup). Combine flour, sugar, baking soda, salt and cinnamon in large bowl. Add bananas, pineapple with juice, eggs, oil and vanilla. Mix until well-blended. Stir in cherries. Pour into greased and floured 13x9 inch baking pan. Bake at 350 degrees for 30-35 minutes. Cool 30 minutes. Apply frosting.

Frosting

¼ cup butter or margarine

3-4 tablespoons milk

3 cups confectioner's sugar

1 teaspoon vanilla

Heat butter and 3 tablespoons of milk until butter is melted. Remove from heat. Stir in confectioner's sugar and vanilla. Beat until smooth. Add extra tablespoon milk, if needed, while beating frosting. Apply to bars when cooled.

Pecan Tarts

1/2 package cream cheese (4-ounces)

1 cup self-rising flour

1 stick butter

Filling

1 cup chopped pecans

¾ cup brown sugar

1 teaspoon vanilla

2 teaspoons white Karo syrup

1 egg

In bowl, mix together first 3 ingredients to make crust. In a separate bowl, mix together ingredients for filling. Roll enough crust into small 1" balls. Place on cookie sheet allowing space between each ball. Make a hole with thumb in each ball. Put 1 teaspoon of filling into crust balls. Repeat process. Bake at 325 degrees for 25 minutes.

Tip: Toasting pecans, walnuts, or cashews makes them crunchier, deepens their color, & shakes off any staleness.

Strawberry Symphony

1 pint strawberries, hulled

1 envelope Dream Whip topping mix

1/3 cup sugar

¼ teaspoon almond extract

1 pint vanilla ice cream, softened

Using a potato masher or fork, mash strawberries. Prepare whipped topping as directed on package, adding sugar to the mix. Stir in almond extract and ice cream; then stir in strawberries. Pour into an 8 inch square pan. Freeze until firm.

Yields: 10-12 servings

History: In 1947, Reddi Whip was the first major aerosol food product.

Fresh Strawberries with Cream Dip

1   8-ounce package cream cheese, softened

1   cup sour cream

1/3   cup confectioner's sugar

2   teaspoons orange liqueur

1   quart fresh strawberries, washed & hulled

In a small mixing bowl, beat cream cheese, sour cream, sugar, & orange liqueur until smooth, Chill 1 hour. Fill 8 cordial glasses or tiny cups with cream dip. Place each on dessert plate & surround with whole berries. To eat, dip berries in cream.

Servings: 8

Tip: Strawberries should be stored in the refrigerator, caps attached, until ready to use.

Note: 1 cup strawberries=45 calories

Cranberry Squares

1   16-ounce can cranberry sauce

1   3.5-ounce package red Jello, any flavor

2   cups buttermilk

1   8-ounce container Cool Whip

1   cup chopped nuts (2 small packages)

Heat cranberry sauce in a large pan. Add Jello to sauce; stir until dissolved. Remove from heat. Add buttermilk. Stir; let stand until cool. Fold in Cool Whip and chopped nuts. Place in refrigerator until firm. Cut into squares.

Note: Even if you're not a fan of buttermilk, you won't be able to tell that it's in the recipe. The cranberry squares are surprisingly good.

Quick Country Rice Pudding

1 1/3 cups quick cooking rice

2 teaspoons butter

½ teaspoon salt

1 3.9-ounce box vanilla flavor instant pudding

2 cups milk

½ cup heavy cream

¼ teaspoon cinnamon

In a 3-quart casserole dish, put rice, butter, salt, and 1 1/3 cups water. Covered & cook on high for 7-8 minutes in microwave until rice is very tender and liquid is absorbed. Refrigerate 15 minutes to slightly cool. Prepare instant pudding and 2 cups of milk as package directs. Beat heavy cream to soft peaks. Fold pudding, whipped cream, and cinnamon into rice.

Yields: 6 servings

Tip: For a larger volume, chill the beaters & bowl before beating.

CHAPTER 8

Miscellaneous Recipes

Mamaw Stevens deciding what to fix for lunch.

Cookin' Notes

Creamy Gravy

4   tablespoons fat left in skillet plus brown crumbs from fried
      meat
4   tablespoons flour
1   cup cold milk
1   cup water
1/8   teaspoon salt & pepper

Use 4 tablespoons fat plus the brown crumbs from the fried meat in the skillet. In a measuring cup, combine cold milk and flour. Stir with whisk until blended. Heat fat until hot; add flour mixture to fat. Cook for 2 minutes then add 1 cup water, salt, and pepper. Constantly stir gravy. Reduce to medium low heat and cook for 2 minutes. Reduce to low heat. Continue cooking and stirring mixture for 5-6 minutes. May need to add more salt and pepper to taste. Serve hot.

Yields: 3 cups

Giblet Gravy

¼   cup drippings from chicken or turkey
2-3 cups chicken broth
     chicken or turkey giblets, chopped
  3 level tablespoons flour
  1 cup cold water
     salt & pepper to taste
  1 tablespoon butter, optional

In a saucepan, boil giblets in chicken broth until done, approx. 30-40 minutes. Set aside. When cooled, remove giblets & cut into smaller pieces. Return to broth. In a measuring cup, add flour to cold water. Mix thoroughly. Add flour mixture to giblets in saucepan. Continue cooking on medium heat. Stir continuously until reaching desired thickness. May need to add more flour/cold water mixture.
Serve hot.

Yields: 3 cups

Note: Giblets can be prepared ahead of time before making gravy the next day. Be sure to reserve the broth along with the giblets.

Red-Eye Gravy

ham grease (from a thick slice raw ham)

1-2 tablespoons Crisco, if needed

¼ cup water

½ cup coffee

salt & pepper to taste

Cut thick slice from a raw ham. Have the frying pan real hot to brown the ham slice quickly on both sides. After browning, fry slowly until done. If there is not enough fat on the meat to make enough gravy, add some Crisco to the frying pan. When done, pour the grease into a bowl. Return the pan to the stove and heat. Add water to the pan and return the grease. Simmer 8-10 minutes. Add coffee, salt, and pepper. Cook until hot. Serve immediately.

Yields: 1¼ cups gravy

Tip: Coffee will make the gravy browner.

Raisin Sauce for Ham

1 teaspoon flour

1/8 teaspoon salt

¼ cup brown sugar

½ cup orange juice

½ cup water

2 teaspoons vinegar

1/3 cup raisins

Mix first 6 ingredients together on medium heat until thick. Add raisins. Cook until well blended and hot. Pour over ham the last 30 minutes of the baking process.

Hollandaise Sauce

3   egg yolks

1   teaspoon water

1   teaspoon bottled lemon juice

2   sticks butter, melted

    salt to taste

Whisk yolks, water, and lemon juice together. Place in pot and heat on low until warm. Stir in melted butter. Continue heating until warm again. Serve immediately.

Barbecue Sauce

  2   tablespoons butter

¼   cup Worcestershire sauce

½   onion, grated

  1   cup ketchup

1/8   teaspoon salt

  1   teaspoon hot sauce

  1   tablespoon chili powder

  1   clove garlic, minced

¼   cup brown sugar

  1   cup water

  2   tablespoons white vinegar

Melt butter in sauce pan, cook onion until translucent. Add the remaining ingredients and stir well. Simmer over low heat for 40 minutes.

Note: When taking foods off the grill, put them on a clean plate, not the same platter that held the raw meat.

Thousand Island Dressing

1   cup mayonnaise

½   cup ketchup

2   hard boiled eggs, chopped

2   teaspoons minced onions

1   teaspoon bottled lemon juice

Combine all ingredients together. Cover and chill for 2 hours before serving.

Yields: 2 cups

French Dressing

½   cup sugar

¼   cup vinegar

1   cup oil

1   tablespoon Worcestershire sauce

2   tablespoons minced onion

¼   cup ketchup

¼   teaspoon salt

Put all ingredients in blender for 20 seconds. Refrigerate for 2 hours before serving.

Bleu Cheese Dressing

8   ounces bleu cheese, crumbled

1½ cup vegetable oil

1   teaspoon sugar

1   teaspoon salt

½   cup vinegar

½   teaspoon dry mustard

1/8 teaspoon garlic powder

Combine sugar, salt, vinegar, mustard, and garlic powder with 3-ounces of bleu cheese in a bowl. Slowly add oil while mixing with blender. Stir in remaining 5-ounces of bleu cheese. Chill for 2 hours before serving.

Creamy Honey Dressing

½   cup mayonnaise

½   cup sour cream

2   tablespoons bottled lemon juice

1   tablespoon honey

1   tablespoon milk

½   teaspoon cooking oil

Combine all ingredients together. Mix well. Refrigerate 2 hours before serving.

Yields: 1 cup

Tip: 1 pound of honey =1 cup

Russian Dressing

2 cups sugar

1 cup white vinegar

½ cup water

1 teaspoon celery seed

1 teaspoon salt

1 cup vegetable oil

1 cup ketchup

1 teaspoon paprika

1 teaspoon Worcestershire sauce

1 small onion, grated

Cook sugar, water, and vinegar. Cool. Add remaining ingredients. Chill overnight.

Yields: 4 cups

Garlic Vinaigrette

½ cup extra virgin olive oil

1 tablespoon vinegar

½ teaspoon salt & black pepper

2 cloves garlic, finely minced

Combine all ingredients; mix thoroughly. Chill in refrigerator 2 hours before serving.

Yields: ½ cup

Tip: Always make the vinaigrette dressing at least ½ hour ahead of time so the ingredients have time to blend.

Cucumber Dressing

½ cup mayonnaise
½ cup low-fat plain yogurt
½ cup cucumber, chopped
 1 teaspoon chives, chopped
 1 teaspoon parsley flakes
¼ teaspoon salt
¼ teaspoon dill weed

Combine mayonnaise and yogurt; mix thoroughly. Stir in the remaining ingredients. Cover and refrigerate for 2 hours before serving.

Yields: 1½ cups

Buttermilk Dressing

 1 cup buttermilk
½ teaspoon onion juice (use juice from 8-ounce jar cocktail onions)
¾ teaspoon salt
1½ tablespoons bottled lemon juice

Combine all ingredients and mix well. Refrigerate for 2 hours before serving.

Yields: 1 cup

Homemade Fish or Chicken Coating

2/3 cup powdered milk

1 teaspoon poultry seasoning

1 teaspoon granulated chicken bouillon

2 teaspoons paprika

½ teaspoon dry mustard

1 teaspoon salt

Put all ingredients in a large bowl or gallon size plastic bag; mix thoroughly. Rinse fish or chicken; drop individual pieces into coating. Shake to coat evenly.

Note: When frying fish, follow this rule: 10 minutes of cooking for every inch of thickness. Let fish stand for 3-4 minutes before serving so heat & juices have time to redistribute.

Jellied Cranberry Sauce

4 cups cranberries

2 cups water

2 cups granulated sugar

Boil cranberries with water until berries stop popping. Strain through sieve; add sugar and stir. Boil rapidly for 8-10 minutes. Put in a mold. Refrigerate until chilled. Serve as a side dish with beef, pork, or poultry.

Tip: Bounceberry is another name for cranberry because ripe cranberries can bounce. It is helpful to know that cranberries can be frozen for 8-9 months.

Orange Punch

1½ cups sugar

  1 cup water

  2 quart bottles orange soda

  2 quart bottles ginger ale

  1 33.8-ounce bottle Tom Collins mix

  2 46-ounce cans pineapple juice

Boil sugar in water until dissolved; stirring constantly. Cool & mix with other ingredients. Chill before serving.

Serves: 40

Marriage Punch

  8 cups water

  4 cups sugar

  2 16-ounce packages Kool-Aid (not grape)

  2 46-ounce cans pineapple juice

  2 lemons; squeezed & chilled (equals 6 tablespoons juice)

  1 16-ounce can frozen orange juice

  5 bananas, pureed in blender

  1 2-liter bottle 7-Up

  1 6-ounce jar cherries

Bring water, sugar, and Kool Aid to boil for 5 minutes. Set aside to cool. Add the remaining ingredients. Stir well. Freeze. Thaw frozen mixture in a punch bowl. Add large bottle of 7-Up right before serving to guests. Add small bottle of cherries to punch.

Pink Punch

1   46-ounce can pineapple juice

2   cups boiling water

2   3.5-ounce packages strawberry Jello

6   cups cold water

½   cup sugar

1   16-ounce can frozen orange juice

1   12-ounce can frozen lemonade

1   quart ginger ale
    lemon or orange slices

Add boiling water to Jello. Stir until dissolved. Add cold water and juices. Add ginger ale before serving. Garnish punch bowl with slices of lemons or oranges.

Grape Punch

4   2-liter bottles ginger ale, chilled

2   16-ounce cans grape juice

2   16-ounce cans orange juice

6   lemons, juiced (1 cup plus 2 tablespoons)

2   pounds sugar

2   quarts water

Boil lemon juice, sugar, and water. Cool. Add the other juices. Chill. Add ginger ale before serving.

Red Satin Punch

  1   quart apple juice

10   2-liter bottles 7-Up

  2   pints cranberry juice cocktail

Fill 2 ice trays with 7-Up and freeze. Chill the remaining 7-Up. Mix together apple juice and cranberry juice cocktail. Before serving; add the remaining 7-Up. Pour into punch bowl. Empty 7-Up ice cubes into punch.

History: The 1st cranberry crop was harvested in Massachusetts.

Fruit Punch

   6   lemons, juiced (1 cup plus 2 tablespoons)

   1   16-ounce can pineapple juice

   1   16-ounce can grape juice

4½   cups sugar

   2   gallons water

   1   6-ounce jar cherries, optional

Mix lemon juice, pineapple and grape juices together. Melt sugar in water; mix with juices. Put cherries in punch. Chill before serving.

Eggnog

24 egg yolks

2 quarts whipping cream

24 egg whites

2½ cups bourbon

6 tablespoons sugar

18 tablespoons sugar

nutmeg to taste

Beat egg yolks for 20 minutes until fluffy. Continue beating and add bourbon slowly to eggs. Set aside. Whip cream until it stands in peaks. Add 6 tablespoons sugar. Fold egg yolks into whipped cream. Set aside. Beat egg whites until they have lost their gloss. Begin adding the 18 tablespoons of sugar; 1 tablespoon at a time. After all the sugar has been added; continue beating for 10 minutes. Fold the egg whites into the cream and egg yolk mixture. Continue to blend until well-mixed and smooth. Serve in tall glasses with a dash of nutmeg, if desired.

Serves: 25

Tip: Cream will whip better if you add a pinch of salt at the beginning. Sugar should be added half-way through the process.

Homemade Kahlua

6 cups sugar

2 quarts water, divided

2 ounces pure vanilla

1 quart 190 proof grain alcohol

1 ounce instant coffee

Dissolve sugar in 1 quart of hot water. Set aside to cool. Dissolve coffee in other quart of hot water. Set aside to cool. Pour into 1 gallon jar. Add vanilla and alcohol. Set aside for 5 minutes.

Yields: 5 fifths

An Image of My Father, the late Cecil Donald Stevens

As a young child, I remember my dad cooking in the kitchen. He used to have his specialty dishes like fried potatoes (with lots of black pepper), chili, and vegetable soup. To him, cooking was a form of relaxation & gratification. However, Dad's favorite way to relax was to fish. He didn't buy expensive equipment or bait. Dad used night crawlers, minnows, or doughballs. I could always tell when it was time to fish because he was in the kitchen cooking his bait. I know the following recipe isn't edible; but the finished product sure is—bass, trout, or catfish. The "Homemade Fish Coating" recipe in this chapter just might come in handy.

Doughball Recipe

- 2 cups boiling water
- 2 tablespoons vanilla extract
- 2 packages Jello, any flavor
- 2 tablespoons granulated sugar
- 1 cup flour
- 2 cups cornmeal
- 1 cup oats

Bring water, Jello, vanilla, & sugar to a slow boil. Add flour, cornmeal, & oats. Cool. Make into 1" balls. Store in a zipped plastic bag.

CHAPTER 9

Canning Recipes

My dad, Don Stevens, growing vegetables for canning.

Cookin' Notes

Canning Information ~ Jars

Quart jars ~ vegetables, meats, pickles
Pint jars ~ jams, preserves, relishes, sauces
Half-pints ~ jams, jellies, butters, marmalades

Hot Peppers in Ketchup

1   gallon hot peppers
2   32-ounce bottles ketchup
1   pint oil
1   pint white vinegar
1   cup granulated sugar
1   tablespoon salt

Cut off top & bottom of each pepper. Hollow out inside of pepper. Cut into rings. Put in a large pan or bowl; set aside. Put ketchup, oil, vinegar, sugar, & salt into a large pot. Heat until boiling; stir frequently. Put hot peppers in mixture. Heat mixture until boiling restarts. Put mixture into clean jars. Leave 1" head space between mixture & top of jar. Wipe lip of jar with a paper towel before sealing.

NOTE: Be sure to wear heavy rubber gloves before handling hot peppers.

Quarts ~ approx. 6

Pints ~ approx. 9-10

Note: Wesson or Crisco Oil was used when canning these peppers.

Plain Hot Peppers

- 1 gallon hot peppers
- 1 pint white vinegar
- 1 cup granulated sugar
- 1 pint water
- 1 tablespoon alum

Cut off top & bottom of each pepper. Hollow out inside of pepper. Cut into rings. Put in a large pan or bowl; set aside. Put vinegar, sugar, & water into a large pot. Heat until boiling; stir frequently. Put hot peppers in mixture. Heat mixture until boiling restarts. Put mixture into clean jars. Leave 1" head space between mixture & top of jar. Put 1 teaspoon of alum in each jar. Wipe lip of jar with a paper towel before sealing. Seal the jars tightly.

Quarts ~ approx. 6

Pints ~ approx. 9-10

Note: The measurement used for vinegar and water; use ½ of the measurement for the sugar.

Canned Tomatoes

5 pounds ripe red tomatoes
water
pickling salt
bottled lemon juice, optional

Wash tomatoes & remove stems. Place in kitchen sink. Pour boiling water over the tomatoes. Let stand in water for 20 minutes. Drain. Remove skins & quarter in a large bowl. Pack tomatoes into sterilized jars. Insert a knife into each jar to eliminate air pockets. If needed, add more tomato quarters in each jar. Add 1 teaspoon of salt to quarts & ½ teaspoon to pints. Make sure to leave ½" headspace in jars. Wipe jar rims with a paper towel. Place jars in canner or large pot & cover with water. Boiling water should be over the tops of the jars. Frequently ladle hot water over the lids. Boil quarts for 45 minutes and pints for 35 minutes. Using a jar lifter, remove jars to a towel on the kitchen counter. As the jars cool, the lids will seal. Before storing jars in a cool, dark area; make sure that the lids have sealed properly.

Yields: 4 quarts or 8 pints

Notes: May add 1 tablespoon of lemon juice to each quart & 1 teaspoon to pints, if desired.

If using a large pot to can tomatoes; make sure that you place a metal ring in the bottom of the pot before inserting jars. They will get overheated if placed directly on pan's bottom.

Picante Sauce

   5   pounds red tomatoes

   4   small cans chili peppers

   1   teaspoon hot pepper seeds

   1   large onion, diced

   ½   cup green peppers, diced

   1   cup red peppers, diced

   1   clove garlic

   1   6-ounce can tomato paste

   ¾   cup white vinegar

   3   tablespoons sugar

   1   tablespoon pickling salt

   2   teaspoons paprika

   3   tablespoons cilantro, chopped

   1   tablespoon lemon juice per pint

   ½   cup diced mild banana peppers (optional)

Cut top and bottom of tomatoes off. Wash thoroughly. Dice the onions, peppers, and tomatoes and place in a large pan. Add the other ingredients except the cilantro. Cook slowly for 2 hours. Put cilantro in the last 30 minutes. Fill clean jars leaving 1" headspace. Wipe rim of jar with clean paper towel before sealing. Seal tightly. Process in boiling water 20 minutes per pint and 25 minutes per quart.

Yields: 9-10 pints

Tip: Fresh chiles can be stored in the refrigerator for 3 weeks and dried chiles for 4 months.

Bread & Butter Pickles

1   gallon thinly sliced cucumbers

8   small onions, sliced

½   cup salt

Cover the ingredients with ice for 3 hours. Drain well.

Syrup

5   cups sugar

5   cups vinegar

2   tablespoons mustard seed

½   teaspoon cloves

1½ teaspoons turmeric

1   teaspoon celery seed

Mix all ingredients together on medium heat (do not boil). Pack in clean jars. Leave ½" headspace. Wipe jar rim with a paper towel before sealing. Process in boiling water bath for 5 minutes.

Yields: 8 pints

Tip: Add raw cucumbers, carrot strips, green beans & cauliflower to liquid left in pickle jar. Refrigerate for several days & use as cocktail snacks.

Whole Dill Pickles

25 cucumbers
10 fresh dill heads
 5 garlic cloves
 5 hot peppers, halved & seeded (optional)
 5 tablespoons pickling salt

Wash cucumbers. Pack in clean jars. In each quart jar, place 2 dill heads, 1 garlic clove, 1 hot pepper, and 1 tablespoon pickling salt. Bring a mixture of 4 cups cider vinegar and 3 quarts of water to a boil in a large pot. Fill each jar with mixture leaving ½" headspace. Wipe jar rim with a paper towel before sealing. Process in hot water bath for 20 minutes.

Yields: 5 quarts

Tip: Leftover dill pickle juice can be used to clean the copper bottoms of pans.

Canned Okra

  4 pounds small okra pods
2½ teaspoons pickling salt
    boiling water

Remove ends; keep pods whole. Put in a colander & wash thoroughly. Boil for approximately 3-4 minutes. Pack into clean pint jars. Add ½ teaspoon salt & boiling water to each jar; leaving 1″ headspace. Wipe jar rim with paper towel before sealing tightly. Process in hot water bath for 50 minutes. Pressure canner requires 10 pounds pressure for 25 minutes.

Yields: 5 pints

History: Okra was first cultivated in Egypt during the 12th century.

Pickled Corn

3-6 pounds corn
  1 gallon water
 ½ cup sugar
  1 cup pickling salt

Cut corn from the cob. Put the corn in large pot. Add enough water so the corn can be stirred easily with a wooden spoon. Bring to a boil for 5-6 minutes. Let cool. Pack into clean quart jars. In a pan, combine water, salt, and sugar. Cook until salt & sugar dissolve about 10 minutes. Pour hot solution over the corn. Wipe jar rim with paper towel before sealing.

Yields: 4 quarts or 8 pints

Tip: Fry pickled corn in bacon grease or butter. Use as a side dish.

Pickled Beets

1½ cups vinegar
2½ cups water
 1 teaspoon canning salt
 4 cups sugar
 1 teaspoon pickling spice
 ½ bushel red beets

Mix vinegar, water, salt, sugar, and pickling spice together in a large pot. Set aside. Cook beets in water until done. Cool and peel skins. Cut into slices or quarters and put in a large pot. Boil vinegar mixture for 5 minutes. Pack beets into clean pint jars. Pour vinegar mixture over beets leaving ½" headspace. Wipe jar rim with clean paper towel. Seal tightly.

Tip: To make pickled eggs, place hard boiled eggs in leftover beet juice. Store in refrigerator for 2 days before serving.

Crock Pot Apple Butter

 6 pounds apples
3½ cups sugar
 2 teaspoons cinnamon
 1 teaspoon ground cloves

Wash, peel, and core apples. Cook in crock pot on high setting until soft; stirring occasionally. Add sugar, cinnamon, and ground cloves. Cover and cook on high setting for 8-10 hours. Remove lid during the last half hour of cooking. Continue stirring occasionally. Put in clean jars while hot. Leave ½" headspace.

Yields: 4 pints, 2 quarts, or 8 half-pints

Note: Tie a ribbon around the top of the jar & give as an inexpensive gift to friends, relatives, or neighbors.

Processed Apple Butter

6 pounds apples, medium-sized

2 quarts cider

3 cups sugar

2 teaspoons ground cinnamon

¼ teaspoon ground cloves

Wash, peel, and core apples. Cut apples into quarters. Cook in cider about 20 minutes or until tender. Press apples through a sieve. Using 3 quarts of apple pulp, cook in a pot until pulp thickens; stirring frequently with a wooden spoon. Add the spices and sugar. Cook slowly for 1 hour; stirring frequently. Pour hot mixture into clean jars. Leave ½" headspace. Wipe jar rim with paper towel before sealing. Process jars in boiling water bath for 10 minutes.

Yields: 2½ quarts or 5 pints

Note: Allow 2½-3 pounds of apples for each quart.

Chow Chow Relish

12   green peppers

6   cups sugar

12   red peppers

4   cups vinegar

1   small head cabbage

1   teaspoon celery seed

4   cups onions

2   tablespoons mustard seed

4   cups green tomatoes

1   tablespoon turmeric

Soak green tomatoes in water with a ½ cup salt for 3 hours. Drain & rinse tomatoes well. Finely chop all vegetables. Put in a large bowl & mix thoroughly. Put vegetable mixture into clean pint jars. Set aside. Put in a saucepan 6 cups sugar, 4 cups vinegar, 1 teaspoon celery seed, 2 tablespoons mustard seed, and 1 tablespoon turmeric. Mix thoroughly. Cook for 5 minutes until bubbling hot. Pour mixture over vegetables in the jars; leaving ½" headspace. Wipe jar rim with clean paper towel. Seal tightly.

Yields: 6-8 pints

Banana Pepper Relish

½ gallon banana peppers

4 large onions

1 pint vinegar

2 cups sugar

3 tablespoons salt

Finely chop peppers and onions. Put chopped vegetables in a pan. Cover with water and boil for 6 minutes; drain. Add vinegar, sugar, and salt to vegetables. Boil ingredients for 6 minutes. Stirring frequently. Put in clean pint jars. Wipe jar rim with a clean paper towel before sealing.

History: The process of sealing cooked food was developed in France in 1809.

Refrigerator Cranberry-Apple Relish

1 large orange, seeded & quartered

1 large apple, finely chopped

4 cups cranberries

1 tablespoon lemon juice

1¼ cups light brown sugar

½ cup chopped walnuts

¼ teaspoon ground cinnamon

Put orange, cranberries, and apple in a blender. Chop finely. Put in a bowl. Add the remaining ingredients. Transfer to a sealed container. Refrigerate.

Yields: 1½ quarts

Vegetable Relish

- 4   tomatoes, chopped
- 2   teaspoons mixed pickling spices
- 2   small onions, chopped
- ½   cup sugar
- 2   green peppers, chopped
- 1   teaspoon horseradish
- ½   head cabbage, shredded
- 1   cup vinegar
- 2   tablespoons salt

Put chopped vegetables & shredded cabbage in a large saucepan. Add spices in a cheesecloth bag & tie tightly; drop in pan. Combine sugar, horseradish, & vinegar & pour over vegetables until blended thoroughly. Bring to a boil then reduce heat and simmer for 20 minutes or until vegetables are done. Pack into clean pint jars. Wipe jar rim with a paper towel before sealing. Process in hot water bath for 15 minutes.

Yields: 5 pints

Suggestion: Serve as a small side with barbecued chicken or ribs.

Strawberry Jam

3   pints strawberries, chopped

8   cups granulated sugar

1   1.59-ounce package pectin

Put jars & lids in a large pot. Cover with water & boil for 10 minutes. Reduce heat. Keep jars & lids in water until ready to fill with juice. Wash & remove stems. Remove top & bottom of each strawberry. Rinse fruit again. Cut into small pieces and put in a large pot. Cover with water; add pectin to water, and cook 10 minutes or until thick. Strain mixture. Put juice in warm half-pint jars. Leave 1/8" headspace. Skim the foam off the top of mixture. Wipe jar rim with a paper towel before sealing.

Yields: 4-5 half pints

Notes: Be sure jars are warm before pouring in mixture or the jars will crack.

Sprinkling cut fruit with Fruit Fresh will keep fruit from browning for 8 hours.

Pour the strained mixture in jars very slowly to lower the foam level.

Raspberry Jam

9   cups raspberries

3   cups sugar

1   1.59-ounce package pectin

Follow the same directions for strawberry jam.

Note: Can use blueberries or blackberries in this recipe.

Grape Jelly

3   pounds Concord grapes

3   cups sugar

1   1.59-ounce package pectin

Remove stems from grapes. Wash and put grapes in a large pan. Crush grapes & cover with water. Bring to a boil; reduce heat & simmer for 10 minutes. Pour mixture into a large bowl. Leave overnight in a cool place to keep crystals from forming. Put jars & lids in a large pot. Cover with water & boil for 10 minutes. Reduce heat. Keep jars & lids in water until ready to fill with juice. Strain mixture into a large pot. Add sugar; stir thoroughly. Boil for 10 minutes; add pectin. Mix thoroughly. Remove from heat. Pour immediately into hot half pint jars. Leave 1/8" head space. Skim any foam that remains. Wipe jar rim with clean paper towel. Seal tightly.

Yields: 6-8 half pints

Note: Grape jelly can be made from frozen concentrated juice or bottled unsweetened grape juice. Follow the same heating & canning procedure.

Frozen Concentrated Grape Juice

3   6-ounce cans

2   cups water

6   cups sugar

1   1.59-ounce package pectin

Bottled grape juice

3   cups unsweetened grape juice

4½ cups sugar

1   1.59-ounce package pectin

Peach Preserves

- 1 quart peaches, pitted & chopped
- 1 pint light Karo syrup
- 4 cups sugar
- 1 1.59-ounce package pectin

Mix together fruit, sugar, syrup & cook for 20 minutes; stirring occasionally. Add package of pectin in mixture. Mix well. Strain mixture. Put into hot sterilized jars. Skim foam from top of fruit mixture, if needed. Wipe jar rim with clean paper towel. Seal immediately.

Yields: 4-5 half pints

Index

LaVergne, TN USA
22 November 2009
164915LV00002B/4/P